A
Gift
for
GRIEF

LOUISE BATES

ISBN 9798354619757

DISCLAIMER

This book is not intended as a substitute for the medical advice of physicians.

The reader should regularly consult a health professional in matters relating to their health and particularly with respect to any symptoms that may require diagnosis or medical attention.

I am not selling myself as a therapist, nor do I pretend to have the cure for grief, because there is no cure.

THIS BOOK IS DEDICATED TO EVERYONE WHO KNEW AND LOVED MATTHEW

Dear Matthew

I say I miss you every day but that doesn't really cut it. You are missing from my world and there are no words to describe how truly difficult it is most days to exist without you. It gets better but getting better has its own pain. I will continue to love you and keep you in my heart forever. I am learning to live alongside the physical absence of you and I will continue to honour your death by supporting others going through the grief journey.

Lots of love, Mum xx

ACKNOWLEDGEMENTS

I would like to express my deep gratitude to my family and friends for proof reading this book, and for giving me valuable feedback and support.

Thank you, Piper, Bill. Ruth, Karen, Jane, Janice and Chris.

TESTIMONIALS / REVIEWS

"Having worked with grieving clients and provided specialist grief trainings for practitioners for many years now, I have seen just how debilitating grief can be. But it always lifts my spirits when wonderful people who have experienced the immense depth of grief come along and help others on their grieving journey. Louise is one of those people, she has written this amazing book from her heart, with truth and honesty in a way that can be of great help to you, in your grief. She has shared her own story and given practical and helpful advice to aid you if you are going through your own grief. I would highly recommend this book".

Janice Thompson MSc. Grief Specialist, EFT & Matrix Reimprinting Practitioner & Trainer, Colour Mirror Practitioner

"I found this book surprisingly difficult to put down and I would recommend it to anyone looking for help coping with grief. The way Louise brings her teachings and learnings into the book is so cleverly and naturally done. I'm sure this book will help many people."

Karl Dawson, Hay House Author, Trainer Director EFT & Matrix Reimprinting Academy

"This book comes with so much love and although Louise is an expert therapist it feels like it's been written by a friend holding your hand and guiding you gently with no judgment whatsoever. It is informative, very easy to read, gives positive advice, and is relatable. It's intertwined with knowledge, stories, quotes and exercises. This book is not only beneficial to those experiencing grief and loss themselves, but to anyone who wishes to understand grief more, whether for personal or professional reasons."

Kim Marshall, EFT (Emotional Freedom Techniques), Matrix Reimprinting and EDT (Emotional Dousing Technique) Practitioner. Author of, 'How to Kiss Goodbye to Ana: Using EFT in Recovery from Anorexia'.

"Louise skilfully and heart-fully navigates her way around the complexities of Grief. And there are complexities. Normalising grief is one thing, and very important for people who are suffering. However, Louise asserts that a clear path can't be mapped out as everyone's experience of grief is utterly unique. Despite this, I have such a feeling of Louise being alongside, like she really 'gets' it. So this will certainly be my go to book in the future should I need the comfort and solace it so amply provides. It will be a gift to be able to recommend this book to my clients too, when relevant.

A beautiful creation. Thank you, Louise!

Rachel Kent B.Ed, Energetics Psychotherapist, Coach & Trainer

PREFACE - WHY I WROTE THIS BOOK

I have had my share of grief over the years but when my son Matthew died, my world changed forever. I remember being on my knees, completely broken and the pain inside was like no other.

Matthew had just turned twenty-five years of age when he was diagnosed with an aggressive and very rare form of kidney cancer. He died two years later.

The time between his death and his funeral, we were showered with flowers, sympathy cards, texts, messages via social media, telephone calls and letters of support. After the funeral, life took on a very different feeling. People were busy getting on with their lives, the world was still spinning, and we felt alone and isolated in our grief. When we did meet up with other people, it felt awkward because not everyone felt comfortable with us. We appreciate now that they did not know what to say and it was easier to not engage with us. Others maybe left us alone because they probably felt we wanted or needed our own space, so their intentions were good. No one seems to know what to say or what to do under these circumstances but there is nothing anyone can do or say that can make it right.

I fondly remember all the little things that helped me in those early days when grief was all consuming and brutal.

A few weeks after the funeral someone hand delivered a little booklet through our front door. It contained poems and prayers, and it really touched me. Even though I am not a church person, I remember thinking, what a thoughtful gift. I still don't know who posted it.

A few months later the parents of one of Matthew's friends sent us a letter and she included a few photographs she had found of the boys playing together when they were younger. They also included photos of a holiday they had invited him on years before.

Another friend visited on occasions dropping off groceries which was a godsend as shopping was so incredibly hard in the early days.

Sometimes I would open my front door and find random parcels such as, homemade cakes, tins of sweets or chocolates, and flowers with little notes attached reminding us that we were still in people's thoughts.

I will never forget those random acts of kindness which came out of the blue. I am hoping this book will be a lifeline for others going through a difficult journey and maybe this book was gifted to you with the same intention.

My son's death has taken me on a personal journey of self-discovery and I now have a passion to help others. Turning my grief and loss experience into something positive is the way forward for me. I have travelled through the darkest depths of my soul and survived the worst period of my life, and my experience has taught me many lessons which I would like to share with others.

Since Matthew's death, I have embarked on many grief webinars and bereavement training courses. My experience of grief alongside the grief specialist training, gives me the confidence to hold the space for others struggling through bereavement. I feel it is an honour to support this group of people.

I truly believe as a society we need to educate people on how to be around grief and eliminate the clumsiness and unease that currently exists. It is time to stop hiding grief behind closed doors and start talking more openly about it and encourage people to come together and share experiences. We need to create safe places where people can acknowledge their pain and loss, where it will be received with love, compassion and empathy instead of awkwardness. Coming together to share and mourn we can potentially support each other. I believe there is a healing power in solidarity. There are some things you can only share with others going through the same anguish. For some, grief may be a private affair and this too must be respected. I wanted to be private about some aspects of my experience but open about others.

Grief is unique to each person. Your grief will be very different to my grief, but what we do share are the same emotions and sensations. They will come and go at different times and at different intensities, but we connect to each other through our shared grief experience. As you read this book hold that knowledge in your heart to remind yourself that you are never alone.

This book is not about fixing you or forcing the healing process; it is about being there with you, guiding you, supporting you, hearing you, acknowledging your pain and metaphorically holding your hand. I have been in your shoes and walked this path too and I have learned many things along the way. The first thing I would like you to know is that grief cannot be healed; it can only be acknowledged, absorbed, carried, experienced, loved and cared for and I hope this book guides you along this path.

My journey of self-discovery through grief feels like a pilgrimage but also my greatest adventure which will continue until the day I die. It has taken me through my darkest time but at last, I am finding contentment along the way. I have moments of happiness and moments of sadness and all the other emotions in between, but I have discovered a new level of peace, and as I move forward, I intend to be in this space as much as possible.

My hope is that this book guides others who are walking a similar path to seek out their own personal journey of self-discovery and find that life can be meaningful again after the death of a much loved one.

Transformation is an inside job!

INTRODUCTION

If you have been given this book as a gift, keep it close to you. It has been written with love and with an open heart from me to you.

Maybe the title spoke to you, and you bought it for yourself. I am so pleased we connected.

Whether you are newly bereaved or whether you have been stuck in grief for years, I do hope this book brings you some comfort.

First, let me say how incredibly sorry I am for your loss.

Second, let me assure you that you are not alone.

Third, welcome to a club that no-one wants to join.

This grief journey you have been forced to take is not an easy one, but I do hope this book supports you along the way. I hope it shines a light on your path and gives you the strength to navigate your way through the grieving process.

This book contains a compilation of poems, parables, ramblings, affirmations, meditations, exercises and inspirational quotes. They helped me when my son Matthew died and my hope is that they will help you too. I have included musings from my blog posts and uplifting information from my first book, 'Letters to Matthew, Life After Loss'. My hope is that by sharing my experience it will help others too. I have also included some case studies from my work as a therapist.

Reading a book about grief may seem daunting at first and I totally understand. Facing your grief head on can be overwhelming but this is a book to dip in and out of. You can randomly open a page, read a small piece, then close the book. Hopefully that small piece will loosen or lighten your grief in some way.

Grief covers such a large area and what is right for one person may not be right for someone else. Some information in this book may not resonate with you but for others the information may be beneficial. Take what resonates with you and leave the rest. If you do not feel ready for this book, that's okay. Hide it in a cupboard until you do feel ready. Read this book in your own time. You are in control.

If you would like to find out more about my personal story, check out my website.

www.louisebates.co.uk

UNDERSTANDING GRIEF

Grief is a reaction to loss.

The way we experience grief is as individual as a fingerprint or a snowflake.

There are no universal stages to grief.

People will grieve in different ways. Some people may express their grief verbally, some people cry easily, while others channel their grief into activities. Any of these responses are normal; and how we grieve is not a measure of how we love.

There is no timetable to grief. Over time the pain lessens and we return to similar levels of functioning, sometimes even better levels of functioning. I know that nothing can hurt me more than losing my child and I feel I have a superpower. Anything else that life throws at me, I know I can survive because I have survived this.

Accidents, murders, sudden illnesses, tragedies, or medical events unfortunately happen and people die without any warning. Even when the death is expected, the impact can still be devastating. There is no easy way to lose a loved one. Whether you lost your loved one suddenly or whether their death was expected, you never feel that you have had enough time with them. Grief can be brutal and all-consuming in the beginning but understand that it will change. Grief comes in many forms, but the way we deal with grief these days can sometimes be outdated.

In 1969, Elisabeth Kübler-Ross (a famous American psychiatrist who specialised in grief) described the five stages of grief as denial, anger, bargaining, depression, and acceptance. These five stages simplify the bereavement process but in reality, there are no rules.

Since the five stages were first developed, there have been lots of new ways of thinking about grief. There are various models to help us understand bereavement but one I find the most helpful, is the idea of 'growing around your grief.' In this model, there are no set stages or phases. Instead, your grief remains the same, but you grow around it.

Avoid any therapists who claim their five step, or twelve step programmes will transform you. And if anyone tries to help you by referring to the five stages of grief……..make your excuses and get out of there fast!

You will hear people say that time is a healer, but time is not the healer; time is just the vehicle that takes you on your grief journey. You are the healer. How you process your experience of grief and loss determines how quickly you evolve and how soon you grow around it.

Using words like resilience and strength can be annoying. Resilience is about having the capacity to recover quickly from difficulties. Resilience is the ability of a substance or object to spring back into shape. Some people may have more tools for dealing with a stressful situation than others and this may or may not make them more resilient. It's not about being resilient, it's about having access to the right resources and self-help tools. I personally feel resilience is what grows around our grief as we process the experience.

GRIEF POEM

I had my own notion of grief.

I thought it was a sad time that followed the death of someone you love.

And you had to push through it.

To get to the other side.

There is no pushing through.

But rather, there is absorption.

Adjustment.

Acceptance.

And grief is not something that you complete, but rather you endure.

Grief is not a task to finish and move on, but an element of yourself, an alteration of your being.

A new way of seeing.

A new definition of self.

© Gwen Flowers – Printed with permission.

WHAT I'VE LEARNED ABOUT GRIEF

When I was eleven years old the unexpected sudden death of my eldest brother Stephen changed my family forever. To see and hear my parents so distraught seemed more upsetting to me than the sad fact that my brother had died. I did not understand death as I had not experienced it before and I only saw him last night, so how could I miss him?

What I remember most about that time, was how upset other people were. The constant flow of crying visitors with their kind words and sympathies seemed never-ending for days, so I knew this was big stuff, but I didn't understand it. (Our family didn't have a phone at the time and it was before the internet was invented, so visiting was one of the only ways people could pass on their condolences).

This was the only time in my life that I wanted to go to school. I believed that school would be an escape away from all the sadness that had taken over my home life. This experience taught me that adults find dying incredibly sad and it was not until I was much older that I really started to understand the grief I felt for my brother.

Grief has visited me a few times since then due to other losses, but when my son Matthew died, the pain of his loss took me to a new level of sadness. For a while, I created self-tormenting programmes and thoughts such as, "what if?" or "if only?" I found myself focusing on the last few months of illness and the negative memories associated with Matthew's death. I also worried that if I stopped grieving, it would mean I no longer cared or loved Matthew anymore.

I created distractions and started painting and decorating the house. Some people throw themselves into work as a way of dealing with their grief while others may choose to over eat or sit and watch the television all day. Healthy distractions may be beneficial for a while, but I would be mindful that there are also various unhealthy distractions such as smoking or drinking too much or taking drugs. Unhealthy distractions may dull the pain for while, but you need to feel it to heal it and these habits can be difficult to stop.

Our ancestors were more familiar with death because so many of their children died young. That does not mean their grief was any easier, but they had more practice and they knew how to grieve. If we are lucky, in the western world, we can go through most of our lives and not experience grief.

Family, society and religion can only do so much with their well-meaning ways, but they are not equipped to deal with the rawness of overwhelming sorrow and grief. The British in particular have an unhelpful attitude to grief with their stiff upper lip and '*keep calm and carry on*' approach. Phrases like, "*keep your chin up*", "*don't mope about*", "get over it", "*your loved ones wouldn't want you to be sad*", "*you need to move on*" etc. are not what you want to hear.

I have learned that grief is not a state on its own but a combination of different emotions such as anger, sadness, guilt, etc. It harbours pain, shock, trauma, anxiety, overwhelm, confusion and even feelings that have no label.

There are no rules to bereavement but there are many aspects that can influence a person's experience including their belief system, personality type, culture, background and maybe their previous experiences of grief.

It is easy to turn a happy memory of your loved one into a sad one by attaching the sadness you feel from your present-day grief, onto that happy memory, even though, when that happy memory was created, you were not grieving.

It is possible to remember the good memories without the sadness of the present-day grief, but only we can make that happen. No one else can do this for us. These memories are the gifts they have left behind for us to keep. You can honour your loved ones by connecting and remembering the good times, the laughter, the smiles, the special moments because this will send them peace beyond belief.

Grief often rearranges your relationships. Some people will stay with you for the ride and others may fade away.

Nothing anyone says is going to make you feel better but if others ignore your grief, because they feel awkward, or they don't know what to say, or they think it will make you worse, this hurts even more.

I quite often get asked, what is the best thing to say to someone who is grieving? I wish I knew the right answer to this. What you say to one person may be just what they need to hear but for others it may be a clumsy throwaway comment. It also depends on the type of relationship you have with the person. If you say something like, "I'm here if you need anything," would maybe sound weird if you barely knew the person, but saying, "I'm sorry for your loss" may not be right if it's someone very close to you.

My answer to this question is, don't try to fix something that cannot be fixed and grievers do not want to be rescued. Acknowledge their grief in some way, even if it feels awkward or sounds clumsy, say something. Let them know you can see the landscape they are in. You can encourage them to talk and really listen, but if they do not want to talk, ask them, "Is it okay if I keep checking in with you?"

You could also send a card, a letter, a text, an email, flowers, bake a cake, etc. Acknowledge their grief in some way.

You can always finish off a message by saying, 'no need to reply if you don't want to'. Giving them permission to stay quiet takes the pressure off them replying.

"If I had a flower for every time I thought of you, I could walk in my garden forever." Alfred Lord Tennyson

TIME IS NOT A HEALER

Many of us have been to the funeral of an elderly or distant relative or maybe the funeral of a colleague or old friend. We have been touched by the sadness felt by their loved ones left behind, but we cannot truly comprehend the brutality of grief until it is our turn to sit on the front pew at the funeral. Nobody can prepare us for when death steals our loved one.

It is often said that some people never get over their loss. I know of people who have lost a loved one and are still angry five years afterwards and others who are still broken decades later. If time was the healer, why are these people still feeling the rawness of grief after so long?

How we process our grief determines how we evolve and steer our way through bereavement.

Nothing could have prepared me for the brutality of grief when my son Matthew died. The early days, weeks and months were incredibly hard, but I kept reassuring myself that it would not always be like that. Each day, no matter how bad I felt, I forced myself to get up, shower and get dressed and I slowly navigated my way through the first stage of grief; that brutal and all-consuming darkness that nothing and no-one can prepare you for. Some days I would take one pace forward and then the next day ten paces back. It was a constant uphill struggle.

Moving Forward

When we talk about bereavement, the phrase 'moving on' is often mentioned, but there is no magic moment when we decide to do this. Also, moving on means leaving it behind, it's over, it's in the past, it's done, but grief doesn't work like that. It is not something you can dump when you have had enough. It is constantly there, pulling at your heart strings. Over time grief does weaken, but time is just the vehicle that navigates you along the journey. How you process grief determines the rate at how fast or slow you evolve. It is different for everyone, but it never goes away. There is NO moving on!

Moving forward is a much softer and realistic way to explain how grief ebbs and wanes.

Moving forward is about carrying the grief and learning to coexist with it.

I will carry my grief with me till the day I die, but I will continue to move forward in the best way I can.

It's time to trust yourself.
Forgive yourself.
Be gentle with yourself.
Listen to yourself.
No-one else can do this for you.

GETTING OVER GRIEF

Your precious irreplaceable loved one is gone from this world, and you cannot help but constantly miss them.

Six months, one year, two years, three years, five years, ten years, twenty years……….
There is no getting over it!
You grow to accept it.
You grow around it.
You carry it carefully and lovingly wherever you go.

You have strategies to contain it even though it sometimes leaks out of your eyes without warning.

You give yourself permission to cry in certain places maybe the shower, the garden, the kitchen, the car.

The loss of a loved one is permanent.
There is no getting over it!

Your life is different now, but grief does not have to define you and you do not need to feel like a victim.

Grief may have the potential to create a deeper strength and meaning to your life and there could be positives. There is a gift in everything. You will have moments of happiness, you may laugh at something funny, you may see the beauty in a flower, maybe you can enjoy a cup of coffee - but that does not mean you are over it.

There is no getting over it!

Life is – laughter and tears, delight and defeat, joy and sorrow.

GRIEF IS LIKE A SHIPWRECK

As for grief, you'll find it comes in waves.

When the ship is first wrecked, you're drowning, with wreckage all around you.

Everything floating around you reminds you of the beauty and the magnificence of the ship that was and is no more. And all you can do is float.

You find some piece of the wreckage and you hang on for a while. Maybe it's some physical thing.

Maybe it's a happy memory or a photograph. Maybe it's a person who is also floating. For a while, all you can do is float. Stay alive.

In the beginning, the waves are a hundred feet tall and crash over you without mercy. They come ten seconds apart and don't even give you time to catch your breath. All you can do is hang on and float.

After a while, maybe weeks, maybe months, you'll find the waves are still a hundred feet tall, but they come further apart. When they come, they still crash all over you and wipe you out. But in between, you can breathe, you can function.

You never know what's going to trigger the grief. It might be a song, a picture, a street intersection, the smell of a cup of coffee. It can be just about anything…and the wave comes crashing. But in between waves, there is life.

Somewhere down the line, and it's different for everybody, you find that the waves are only eighty feet tall. Or fifty feet tall. And while they still come, they come further apart.

You can see them coming. An anniversary, a birthday, or Christmas. You can see it coming, for the most part, and prepare yourself.

And when it washes over you, you know that somehow you will again, come out the other side. Soaking wet, sputtering, still hanging on to some tiny piece of the wreckage, but you'll come out. Take it from an old guy. The waves never stop coming and somehow you don't really want them to. But you learn that you'll survive them. And other waves will come. And you'll survive them too. If you're lucky, you'll have lots of scars from lots of loves. And lots of shipwrecks.

MEANINGFUL WAYS TO HONOUR YOUR LOVED ONE

When a loved one dies, it is natural to worry about losing the memories we have of them. We will never forget the person they were to us, but it is helpful to find solid ways to honour their memory.

Honouring our loved ones with a service helps to bring people together. Friends and family members can grieve alongside one another and show how the deceased positively impacted their lives. It allows us to connect to one another and come together to celebrate the person we all loved. This is a therapeutic process for families and friends of the deceased. There is a healing energy in coming together. Honouring the deceased and paying respects allows us to celebrate a life well lived and share the deceased's story. By sharing your favourite memories, you can make sure your loved one's memory will live on forever with everyone in attendance.

Whether it is the death of a tiny baby or an elderly relative, honouring the life of a loved one can support you to move forward in your life.

Different ways you can honour your loved one:

- Choose a place to remember them
- Create a virtual tribute, video / film
- Turn their ashes into jewellery or an ornament
- Keep their ashes or spread them somewhere special
- Write them a letter
- Experience their favourite things
- Donate their possessions to a charity
- Start a charity
- Watch their favourite film
- Create a grant or scholarship in their name
- Complete their unfinished projects
- Visit a place that was special to them
- Keep something of theirs close by
- Light a candle
- Make their favourite food
- Create a photo collage
- Make a memory box
- Listen to their favourite music
- Plant a tree
- Dedicate a bench in their name
- Make something out of their clothing – a teddy bear, a quilt, or cushion
- Paint a pebble in their memory and leave it in their favourite place, or keep it
- Set them a place at the table on important celebrations, their birthdays or at Christmas
- Look at their photos
- Write a journal
- Get a tattoo
- Buy a piece of jewellery in their memory

- Create a space in your home, a shelf or altar for their photographs - add candles, and flowers.
- Keep a lock of their hair

Remember the love they brought into your life.

BODY SCAN MEDITATION FOR RELAXATION

This is normally done in the sitting position. Some people like to record this on their phone so they can listen and follow the guided narration.

Find a comfortable position and place your hands on your lap.

And when you feel ready, lower your gaze, or allow your eyes to close.

Allow your body to be still, sitting upright with a straight back.

Notice any sounds outside the room.

Notice any sounds within the room.

And become aware of the space around you.

Observe the temperature of the space around you.

And now become aware of your breath as it enters and leaves your body.

Breathing through your nose notice the physical sensations with each breath - letting the breath be just as it is - without trying to change it in any way - allowing it to flow easily and naturally - with its own rhythm and pace.

As you sit in your chair – with a straight back - become aware of any tension you may be holding onto – and give yourself permission to let it go - allow your body to feel relaxed – with each out breath – just let it go.

Feel your head become heavy with relaxation – notice the tiny muscles around your eyes and your face – and soften these muscles – feel the muscles in your neck and shoulders – releasing and let go.

Relax your arms and hands, right down to your fingertips. Notice how heavy they have become.

Relax your chest and tummy muscles – and feel the muscles in your back start to loosen.

Relax your hips and your thighs - and feel the heaviness of relaxation travel down your legs. Down and down. Down to your ankles – into your feet – and down to the tips of your toes.

Your whole body is now feeling heavy with relaxation – notice how good it feels.

You may feel yourself drifting into a safe, quiet place.

Feeling relaxed from the top of your head to the tips of your toes.

Pause

Now imagine a white healing light above your head.

You can almost feel the energy of this white healing light.

Visualise in your mind's eye this white light coming into the top of your head - healing and cleansing as it moves down – down through your head and into your throat and neck– feel the healing energy as it moves into your chest - the top of your arms –healing and cleansing – down into your hands – into your tummy - moving down through your body - down and down into your legs – down into your feet – imagine this healing light now leaving your body through the tips of your toes – and going into the earth – leaving you feeling grounded – calm –at peace – sit with this energy for a couple of minutes.

Pause

And now it is time to come back.

As you bring this meditation to a close, start to wiggle your fingers and toes.

Notice the space around you.

Notice any sounds in the room.

Feel your body sat on the chair.

Become aware of your feet touching the floor

When you feel ready - open your eyes.

This meditation can be downloaded for FREE from my website.

DEATH IS NOTHING AT ALL

Death is nothing at all.
I have only slipped away to the next room.
I am I and you are you.
Whatever we were to each other, that, we still are.
Call me by my old familiar name.
Speak to me in the easy way which you always used.
Put no difference into your tone.
Wear no forced air of solemnity or sorrow.
Laugh as we always laughed at the little jokes we enjoyed together.
Play, smile, think of me. Pray for me.
Let my name be ever the household word that it always was.
Let it be spoken without effect.
Without the trace of a shadow on it.
Life means all that it ever meant.
It is the same that it ever was.
There is absolute unbroken continuity.
Why should I be out of mind because I am out of sight?
I am but waiting for you.
For an interval.
Somewhere. Very near.
Just around the corner.
All is well.

Nothing is past; nothing is lost.
One brief moment and all will be as it was before only
better,
infinitely happier and forever we will all be one
together with Christ.

Henry Scott Holland

YOU ARE GRIEVING – TRANSFORMING

Do you remember what life was like before your loss? Maybe it was perfect or maybe it was flawed, but whatever it was - it was probably much better than this. Going to work, the supermarket, the hairdressers, socializing and all the other normal everyday activities now seem like huge mountains to climb.

Your life has changed forever and it will change you. You are not only grieving the loss of your loved one, but you are also missing your life, the life you had when they were part of it.

Part of your grief experience is coming to terms with how it changes you. We unconsciously try to hang onto the person we were before the loss because that is what we know, it is our natural default setting. Maybe we resist these changes because it feels like we will lose that connection to our loved one. Maybe it is easier to stay the same because change feels uncomfortable. We do like the safety of our comfort zones.

When we allow ourselves to transform through the process, we can begin to move through the bereavement journey. If not, we can easily become stuck. Moving through the process is honouring our loved ones. It doesn't mean we love them any less or that we are forgetting them - we are carrying them forward with us. Nothing will ever take that bond away.

Is it time to celebrate the life of your loved one and accept the gift of your own life still to be lived?

I AM TRANSFORMING

2014 was a life-changing year for me. I was in a place where I felt happy with my relationships, I was content in my work as a complementary therapist, and I was a proud mum of two incredible human beings. My daughter had already flown the nest and my son was about to fledge and I was looking forward to a new era with my hubby Bill when it would be just the two of us again. We could have romantic meals without being disturbed and the house would stay tidy. Our future was looking even more exciting! I was in a great place mentally, emotionally, physically, and spiritually. My life was perfect, and my mantra was, *"How much better can it get?"*

I call those days BC – Before Cancer.

I also remember thinking, 'What if?' What if something comes along and spoils my happiness? I was worried that there was something dark just around the corner. I confided in a spiritual friend that I could feel a shift occurring. I could sense the ground shaking beneath me, and it was as if something inside me knew what was coming. Dr. Brene Brown explains that *'joy is the most difficult and terrifying emotion because when we lose our tolerance for vulnerability, our joy becomes foreboding'*. I kept putting any insecure thoughts out of my mind knowing that everyone gets these insecure thoughts from time to time, but deep inside I knew. I could feel it!

Later that year my son was told he had stage 4 papillary renal cell carcinoma – he had cancer – and in that moment, our worlds collapsed. This was followed by over two years of anguish, anxiety, fear, operations, endless medical stuff and we learned new words like 'scanxiety'. During this time, I looked at anything that could potentially support Matthew's recovery and I became 'a mum on a mission'.

I meditated, I wrote affirmations, I used crystals, reiki, reflexology, EFT, etc. I asked the universe to guide me. I researched the best foods to eat, the best supplements to take, the best treatments to have. I juiced vegetables, I sourced illegal cannabis oil, I begged the angels and God to heal my son. In fact, I investigated every alternative and complementary protocol out there to save him. These things worked for some people so maybe they could work for my son too. Unfortunately, nothing worked and Matthew died on the afternoon of Friday 28th October 2016 aged 27 years of age.

I call these days AD – After Death.

I often think about my 'mum on a mission days' in search for the cure. I had left no stone unturned in my pursuit and nobody else could have tried harder to keep my son alive. Why should I now trust in any alternative or complementary protocol or the universe or the angels or God again, because they didn't help?

Well today, I still meditate. I continue to practise my positive affirmations. I still believe in crystals, reiki, reflexology, EFT etc. I continue to eat healthily and I still talk to the universe. The illegal cannabis oil is all gone and……..I still believe in the angels and God or some sort of higher power, but 'the mission' is over. I have a deeper understanding now that Matthew's journey was not something I could control and that was hard to accept. I live in hope that his journey and eventual death was maybe part of a soul contract arranged between us before we were born. Perhaps other people close to Matthew were part of that soul group too and we came here for this ride.

I am learning that life is as it should be.
I am learning to trust that all is well.
I am still learning.
I am not grieving – I am transforming.

Stronger Than You Know

Every time you feel inside like you can't go on,
Every time you close your eyes and picture evils won,
Every time a storm rolls by and winds they feel too strong,
Hold on, you're stronger than you know, hold on.

From the album, Fightback by Matthew Bates

WHAT IS DYING?

A ship sails and I stand watching till she fades on the horizon,
and someone at my side says, *"She is gone"*.
Gone where?
Gone from my sight, that is all.
She is just as large as when I saw her.
The diminished size and total loss of sight is in me, not in her,
and just at the moment when someone at my side says,
"She is gone", there are others who are watching her coming,
and other voices take up the glad shout, *"there she comes!"*
And that is dying.

Adapted from the original poem by Rev. Luther F. Beecher 1904

A LETTER TO YOUR LOVED ONE

Writing a letter to your loved one is a very healing act and one of the many ways to help process grief and loss.

We are all haunted by the 'what ifs' and 'if only' thoughts that follow the death of a loved one and is there ever enough time to tell them everything we want them to know? If we could just have one more conversation or one more moment, what would we say? What would we do? Writing to your loved one gives you the space to make this happen.

Writing to Matthew was incredibly therapeutic for me. It not only created a healthy connection to him, but it also stopped me focusing on the loss and emptiness of my grief experience. I wrote over a hundred letters which you can read in my book, Letters to Matthew, and each one helped me to process my thoughts and feelings.

I do not write letters anymore because I now talk to him as if he is still here. I know you probably think I am bonkers, but he is still part of my life and he always will be. Perhaps some people will see that as, not letting him go, or that I have not accepted his passing, but that is not true. For me it is about acknowledging there is only physical death and that his consciousness lives on.

If you would like to write a letter to your loved one, I recommend choosing a time when you will not be disturbed. Create a sacred space by lighting a candle and place a photograph of your loved one on the table. You could also add a personal item such as their watch or an item of their clothing, but if you have not got any personal items or a photograph, a candle will suffice.

Make yourself a drink, sit down with a pen and writing paper and take some slow deep cleansing breaths in and out. You may like to play some of their favourite music, or you may prefer to sit in the silence. Do what feels right for you. Tune into your thoughts and feelings and think about what you would like to say to your loved one. Imagine they have just moved away and they live at a different address now called heaven or angelville or paradise or infinite consciousness; whatever works for you. If you do not believe in an afterlife, you can still write them a letter. There are no rules!

Tell them how much you love and miss them. Explain how hard it has been since they left. If you are angry, tell them. If you are broken and in pieces, tell them. Tell them everything. Nobody else needs to read this letter. It is an intimate and loving act between you and your loved one.

Writing down your thoughts and feelings may seem awkward at first but allow the words to just flow. Tell them how proud you are of them and explain how much you have grown and changed. Tell them how you continue to honour their memory. Explain how they are still part of your life and always will be. Nobody can break the bond you share. When your letter is finished, read it out loud and imagine your loved one is with you and allow your emotions to flow.

What you do with your letter after this is up to you. You can burn it, or you can keep it under your pillow or maybe choose your favourite photograph of them and slip it in the back of the frame. The choice is yours.

"Your name is upon my tongue, your image is in my sight, your memory is in my heart, where can I send these words that I write?"
Rumi

THE POEM – IF

If you can keep your head when all about you are losing theirs and blaming it on you.

If you can trust yourself when all men doubt you but make allowance for their doubting too.

If you can wait and not be tired by waiting, or being lied about, don't deal in lies,

Or being hated, don't give way to hating, and yet don't look too good, nor talk too wise.

If you can dream, and not make dreams your master.

If you can think, and not make thoughts your aim.

If you can meet with Triumph and Disaster and treat those two impostors just the same.

If you can bear to hear the truth you've spoken, twisted by knaves to make a trap for fools.

Or watch the things you gave your life to, broken, and stoop and build 'em up with worn-out tools.

If you can make one heap of all your winnings and risk it on one turn of pitch-and-toss,

and lose and start again at your beginnings and never breathe a word about your loss.

If you can force your heart and nerve and sinew to serve your turn long after they are gone,

And so, hold on when there is nothing in you except the Will which says to them: 'Hold on!'

If you can talk with crowds and keep your virtue, or walk with Kings, nor lose the common touch.

If neither foes nor loving friends can hurt you, If all men count with you, but none too much.

If you can fill the unforgiving minute with sixty seconds' worth of distance run,

Yours is the Earth and everything that's in it, and which is more, you'll be a Man, my son!

Rudyard Kipling

THE AWKWARDNESS OF GRIEF

Someone said, *"I don't know how you do it."* I said, *"I wasn't given a choice."*

Grief is a lonely journey for the griever no matter how much support is offered. It is a unique experience, and nobody can fully comprehend the internal pain and suffering each person goes through. Bereavement forums, grief books, blogs, and websites are a lifeline for people like us. They provide a safe place for the things we cannot share with the rest of the world; a haven where we can safely disclose our thoughts and feelings with others who understand. I feel like I belong to an exclusive club where we can feel comfortable with each other's grief.

I have had people cross the road to avoid me. I understand that they probably felt so uncomfortable with my loss, that it was easier for them to cross the street and pretend to not see me. Maybe they did not know what to say, or do, and they feared they may make me feel worse. I appreciate that their intentions were good!

Maybe it is about time we all had an honest conversation about grief by talking about the clumsiness and awkwardness that surrounds it.

It is no one's responsibility to make the griever feel better. In fact, nothing anyone says will make them feel better, but the worst thing people can do, is ignore it.

(Whatever you do, if you know someone who is grieving, acknowledge their grief. It might make you feel uncomfortable and awkward, but that is nothing compared to what the griever would feel if you ignored it.)

As a society we are getting much better at talking about mental health issues but when it comes to grief and loss, people want us to do that behind closed doors, privately. No wonder some people do not know how to engage with it!

I appreciate that people feel awkward around grief, and this can prevent them from reaching out. Conversations do not have to focus on the pain and sadness of bereavement. We can share good memories and remember the funny, happy times. We can talk about the triumphs of life despite our loss. We can discuss how we honour our loved ones. It does not have to feel uncomfortable and clumsy. What makes a great friend is someone willing to overcome the awkwardness and connect with you. Communication is the key to being kind and compassionate.

Do you know someone who has lost a very important person in their life? Are you afraid to mention their name in case you make them feel sad? You cannot make them feel sad because they are already sad. When you mention their name, you are remembering that they lived and that is a comfort and a great gift.

If we do not mention their names they have a second death, a social death.

"I can no longer see you with my eyes or touch you with my hands, but I will feel you in my heart forever."
Author unknown

CHRISTMAS GRIEF

I appreciate just how difficult Christmas can be for those missing their loved ones. My son Matthew died just two months before Christmas, and it now feels like a time to endure rather than enjoy.

Christmas was a massive event in our family. It was the one time of the year when we really splashed out. Our family had many traditions, but when Matthew died our traditions died too because they could not continue without him. People may find it strange that we do not decorate the house anymore but just the thought of doing this makes me feel emotional. Our old plastic tree and box of decorations and Christmas lights now lie dormant, covered in cobwebs in the attic. People sometimes ask, "why don't you just put out a few Christmas ornaments?" If they were in our shoes, they would know the answer to that question!

We celebrate Christmas differently now. We get on a plane and travel off to warmer climes and enjoy some warm mid-winter sunshine. We sit on the beach wearing our Christmas hats, drinking, and reminiscing on our past Christmases. We remind each other of the funny, happy, special times and we shed a few tears too, but that is okay, it's our new normal. We swim in the sea, relax, sunbathe, and enjoy our new tradition. We also like to find a church and light a candle in his memory. One of the positives about this new tradition means, there is no mad supermarket last minute shopping to do. I do not miss the craziness of the roads when it seems like everybody is out panic buying. I do not miss the cold grey days and disappointment of another Christmas without snow. I do not miss the anxiety of making sure everyone has a perfect day. I do not miss the awful Christmas television programmes. We celebrate Christmas differently now and it feels good to make new traditions.

Our daughter is also creating new traditions with her partner, but we always have a day together when we swap presents before we fly off.

Here are some tips that will hopefully help you get through the festive period if you are missing a loved one:

- Create new traditions in their memory like making a memorial ornament, wreath, or other decoration. In my spare time I like to paint pebbles and I paint a Christmas pebble and take it away with me. I leave it for others to find and then it can be posted on Facebook #letterstomatthew.co.uk
- Decide where you want to spend Christmas. We choose to go somewhere warm and sunny as part of our new tradition, but it may comfort you to stay at home. Wherever you choose to be, maybe light a candle on Christmas day in memory of your loved one. I like to take a photo of Matthew in a frame away with us and it gives me a lot of comfort to light a candle and focus on the joy he

brought into my life. It feels good to have a moment of silence during the festivities. I also like to journal, meditate, and listen to his music.

- Instead of spending money on presents, maybe think about donating to a charity in their name. Explain to your friends and relatives that this is a new tradition. We choose not to send cards anymore as we prefer the money to go to a worthy cause. Each year we donate to a charity that supported Matthew in some way throughout his illness journey.

- Leave an empty seat at the dinner table in memory of your loved one. If we were at home over the Christmas period, I would do this. I would put his photograph on his place setting.

Do not feel guilty if you skip or minimise on the decorations. I don't!

You never know what may trigger a cryfest, but tears are okay. Tears are just love in liquid form and with Christmas everywhere tears are never far away. Others may see our tears as a problem that needs fixing or that we are not coping well but what they do not realise is that tears help us wash away our pain.

Christmas can be tough but remember to enjoy yourself. Would your loved one be mad at you if you did not look for the love, laughter and joy during this period?

Give yourself permission to be happy and remember this does not diminish how much you love and miss your loved one.

I hope you find peace in your heart at Christmas. That is the greatest gift!

The memories they leave behind make the best Christmas presents.

NEW YEAR RESOLUTIONS FOR GRIEVERS

For some people, a New Year traditionally means a fresh start, a new diet or maybe joining a gym, but for others in the midst of grief, a New Year can bring a tsunami of mixed emotions. A New Year feels different for those who are grieving.

I recall how the first New Year without my son completely overwhelmed me. He had only been gone two months but also 'last year', and that sounded so far away. I was entering a New Year without him and the sadness I felt was immeasurable.

I remember hearing the New Year's Eve fireworks going off in the distance and thinking about all the people out partying, while at the same time feeling the enormity of my loss. Outside my experience of grief, the world was still spinning, people were out celebrating, and life continued without my son. Now, as another New Year begins, I add it to the list of years spent without him.

It does not matter how long it's been; grief will emerge when we least expect it. Grief changes us. We do our best to resist that change, believing that the answer to getting through the pain and loss is to try and remain the same.

We try and hold on to the person we were before the loss.

When we allow ourselves to let the experience of grief and loss shape and change us, we grow with it rather than against it. You may feel that this is impossible. Your loved one has died, and your heart is broken. Each day is a struggle and you feel drained with overwhelming emotions. Remember that in this moment – you are alive, your heart is beating and you do have a future. You may never get over your loss but in order for you to move forward you need to release the idea that you can remain unchanged.

Is it possible for you to make peace with your grief this year?

Here is my take on New Year Resolutions for grievers:

- Allow grief to be part of your New Year
- Give yourself permission to be happy
- Be gentle with yourself
- Remember the good memories
- Speak their name
- Spend more time in nature
- Drink more water – tears may dehydrate you
- Live more in the moment
- Meditate
- Listen to music
- Watch comedies
- Journal
- Find a good listener
- Honour your feelings
- Give yourself time to grieve

MEMORIES

My all-time favourite memory is of a family holiday on a beach when our children were young. When I think about it now, I am back there amid the sights and sounds and seaside smells. I can time travel and relive that wonderful time in my life once again. Over time memories are destined to fade but we can keep them alive by just practising them through our thoughts using our imagination. I practice this one quite often!

Memories can be good or bad depending on the experience at the time they were made. They are mainly stored in the hippocampus, the emotion centre and the prefrontal cortex at the very front of the brain.

For quite a while after Matthew's death these good memories were a trigger for me and I could be bought to my knees just by thinking about them. They were almost as painful as the bad memories. When grief is new and raw it seems like everything is a trigger but as we start to grow around our pain we build in resilience and strength.

Even now I can still be consumed with sadness when I think about my good memories, but I am learning to interrupt the process now. When those good memories were made, there was no sadness – Matthew was alive and it was a happy time, but grief has a sneaky way of attaching itself to these good memories.

The best way to deal with this is to fully immerse yourself into the memory. When you think about a memory of your loved one, are you observing yourself in the memory or are you in that memory? If you are observing yourself in the memory your mind can alter, delete, or forget important information. Do not observe your memory - be in that memory. Relive it as if you were looking through your own eyes and smell the smells, hear the sounds, sense the energy now in your body, feel yourself there, be in that moment – in that memory. The deep sorrow you feel from your present-day grief was not part of your life then. This exercise helps you to connect to your loved one in a much healthier way. Remind yourself that the good memories you have of your loved ones are the gifts they have left behind for you to keep.

Go through your photo albums, look at their pictures and feel your loved ones with you. Honour your loved ones by connecting to the love you hold inside for them and remember their smiles, their laughter, remember the good times.

When you fully immerse yourself into this energy you will send them peace beyond belief.

Your intuition knows the way. Follow that feeling.

21 DAY VISUALISATION EXERCISE

Do you feel ready to visit your happy memories?

Caution! You may like to read through this exercise and get a feel for it and think about it first. If you are not sure, or if just thinking about your happy memories trigger you, then skip this exercise. Happy memories can be just as painful as the bad memories sometimes. Maybe today is not a good day but tomorrow may be a better day for you.

If your answer is yes, you do feel ready, then it is safe to continue.

Think about the happiest day in your life.

What is the first thought or image that comes to your mind?

Maybe it is a holiday, or your wedding day, or the birth of your child, or just a special random moment where you felt your happiest.

Go with this memory and do not try and pick another one.

This positive memory came up for a reason.

Now place both your hands on your heart and take two or three deep breaths in and out.

Now picture your positive memory as an image in your mind's eye. (This image could be a picture (photo) or a mini film in your mind).

Imagine you are in the memory now.

Think of any smells that remind you of it.

Hear the sounds of the memory around you now.

Sense the energy of it around you now.

With your eyes closed, imagine you are reliving that memory.

What good emotions and feelings do you feel connected to this memory?

How do these good emotions make you feel? For example: happy, joyful, love, free, bliss, strong, positive, contented, powerful, ecstatic, confident, passionate, enthusiastic, fun, optimistic, grateful, etc.

Where in your body do you feel these good emotions? For example: tummy, heart, chest, head or everywhere. Really connect and relive this happy time.

After a few minutes, take a mental snapshot of this happy memory.

Make this snapshot come into focus and really sharpen the image.

Turn the colours up on your picture.

Make your picture bigger.

Put a frame around your picture.

Bring it closer to you.

Imagine the picture moving into your heart space.

Place both your hands on your heart and push the picture in.

Take two or three deep breaths in and out and relax.

This memory is firmly pressed into your heart space now and you can tap into it anytime.

For the rest of the day, practise this memory on and off. Each day for twenty-one days choose a different positive memory to focus on and practise that chosen memory on and off throughout the day. It takes twenty-one days to create a habit and your twenty-one good memories when practised daily could potentially create inner change.

If you find this exercise helpful, continue after twenty-one days. If you run out of happy memories, recycle your old ones. While you connect to the good memories, your mind cannot differentiate between what is real and what it is you are thinking about. Your mind thinks you are there in the memory and it sends out the feel-good hormones which lift your mood and potentially loosen your grief. Practise your happy memories on and off all day, every day to really gain the benefit. This exercise gives your nervous system a break.

Once the storm is over you won't remember how you made it through, how you managed to survive. You can't even be sure if the storm is over. One thing is for certain. When you come out of the storm you won't be the same person who walked in.

LOOK FOR SIGNS

Do you believe in an afterlife?

"Just when the caterpillar thought the world was over, it became a butterfly." Old proverb

There either is an afterlife or there isn't, nobody really knows but I choose to believe there is something. You do not need to be religious or spiritual to believe this, but it can be a choice whether you do or not.

If you find it hard to consider the possibility of an afterlife, grief may be even more painful. If you have decided that there is no afterlife, and your mind has become set that's fine. (I did not write this book to convert anyone.) Being open minded to all possibilities opens the door to exploration. Once your mind is open, you may start to notice small signs. You may automatically explain it away with your logic or you may intuitively question whether it is your loved one saying "hi". How would you feel about that? Are you ready to open your mind? A curious inquisitive mind is a healthy mind.

Look out for signs around you for example, white feathers. This may be your loved one letting you know they are still around and if you find one in an unusual place that is usually a good sign. These feathers are white and very fluffy.

Become aware the next time you turn on the radio. What are the first words you hear? Is that a message for you? Is there a significance in the song that is playing?

Butterflies signify transformation and I always feel loved ones are near whenever I see one.

I also love cloud gazing too and I quite often see feathers or heart shaped clouds. I have even seen the name MATTHEW written in cloud form. It did not last for long, but it was there in the sky before it morphed into wispy clouds.

Have you ever heard your name being called and thought you imagined it?

Have you ever seen a beam of light that you cannot explain?

Lights in the corner of your eye and even orbs on photographs are said to be spiritual energy. These are all signs that our loved ones are close by.

When a robin redbreast constantly visits you or crosses your path, a loved one in heaven is saying, "*Hello! I'm with you.*"

Some people find old coins in unusual places and they believe this is a sign.

I have felt Matthew around on many occasions. Sometimes it feels like he is giving me a virtual hug and sometimes I just sense him near me. It is always emotional and there seems to be no rhyme or reason to the timing, but I am always grateful for the connection. I have had white feathers appear in unusual places and I have also seen strange lights or orbs. I have had so many experiences over the years that I have no doubt in my mind, there is something after death.

These signs never seem to come when I ask or when I am having a bad day but when they do come it reassures me that his energy is still around. When it happens to you, you will intuitively know. I believe our loved ones live on but in a different dimension. Their physical body has gone but their energy, their essence, their consciousness, is still around.

We experience this physical world through our emotions, time, and our five senses, but our loved one's energy is on a different wavelength. They may not be on our radar, but we are on theirs. If we are open minded, we may notice any signs that come our way. Being open minded makes this possible.

Some people may never get the signs or feel the presence of their loved one and this is hard when you are desperate for a connection. Some people visit mediums or psychics for a slither of information and that may be right for them but not for others. Everyone is different and there is no right or wrong way. Anything that brings you comfort though must be a good thing.

THE TWINS PARABLE

In a mother's womb were two babies.

The first baby asked the other: "Do you believe in life after delivery?"

The second baby replied, "Why, of course. There has to be something after delivery. Maybe we are here to prepare ourselves for what we will be later."

"Nonsense," said the first. "There is no life after delivery. What would that life be?"

"I don't know, but there will be more light than here. Maybe we will walk with our legs and eat from our mouths."

The doubting baby laughed. "This is absurd! Walking is impossible. And eat with our mouths? Ridiculous. The umbilical cord supplies nutrition. Life after delivery is to be excluded. The umbilical cord is too short."

The second baby held his ground. "I think there is something and maybe it's different than it is here."

The first baby replied, "No one has ever come back from there. Delivery is the end of life, and in the after-delivery it is nothing but darkness and anxiety and it takes us nowhere."

"Well, I don't know," said the twin, "but certainly we will see mother and she will take care of us."

"Mother?" The first baby guffawed. "You believe in mother? Where is she now?"

The second baby calmly and patiently tried to explain. "She is all around us. It is in her that we live. Without her there would not be this world."

"Ha. I don't see her, so it's only logical that she doesn't exist." To which the other replied, "Sometimes when you're in silence you can hear her, you can perceive her. I believe there is a reality after delivery and we are here to prepare ourselves for that reality when it comes…"

CHILD LOSS

Speak To Us of Children

And a woman who held a babe against her bosom said, Speak to us of Children.

And he said:

Your children are not your children,

They are the sons and daughters of life's longing for itself.

They come through you but not from you,

And though they are with you yet they belong not to you.

You may give them your love but not your thoughts,

For they have their own thoughts.

You may house their bodies but not their soul,

For their souls dwell in the house of tomorrow,

Which you cannot visit, not even in your dreams.

You may strive to be like them but seek not to make them like you.

For life goes not backward nor tarries with yesterday.

You are the bows from which your children as living arrows are sent forth.

The archer sees the mark upon the path of the infinite,

And He bends you with His might that His arrows may go swift and far.

Let your bending in the archer's hand be for gladness,

For even as He loves the arrow that flies,
So, He loves also the bow that is stable.

Kahlil Gibran.

A WHITE FEATHER

A white feather blown from heaven, settled nearby on the ground.

Found in the most amazing places, letting you know they're still around.
They know a pure white feather, won't fill your soul with fear.

It's just a loving gesture, to let you know they're near.

Don't miss these heavenly feathers, or the comfort that they bring.

They are sent to you with much love, from your loved one's angel wing.

Author unknown

Carry your loss with love.

GRIEF AND RELATIONSHIPS

It is no secret that some marriages and relationships fail after a major loss especially the loss of a child and I completely understand why. The death of a child for example turns your world upside down and changes you. Although you are the same people, you are different and you must get to know each other again under one of the most difficult times imaginable.

After Matthew died, I needed to talk about it, but my husband Bill didn't. I would get upset at random things and Bill would say, *"Why are you getting upset about that?"* I would answer him by asking, *"Why are you NOT getting upset about that?"* We both experienced the loss of Matthew very differently!

I remember saying to him one day, *"You just don't understand,"* and he looked at me and instantly I knew he did understand. We were both hurting inside but showing it in different ways.

Bill's coping strategy was to go to work and keep himself busy. He would look for any distraction to avoid alone time. Sometimes it felt like it was me he was avoiding but he was avoiding being alone with himself.

I wanted deep and meaningful conversations and I wanted to talk about how I felt. I wanted to spend time with Bill and the rescuer in me wanted to help him too. Bill found this very difficult and being busy was an easier option. I know I can be a bit intense sometimes!

Over the years people do change and grow in different directions and break ups are a part of life. We had grown together supporting each other in our various interests and we became more in love with each other with every passing year but when Matthew died, we found ourselves in this new vortex of high emotions. We could not support ourselves let alone support each other. After a while, I noticed we were just going through the motions. We were both so wrapped up in our pain we stopped reaching out to each other. Going through grief together felt like a blessing and a curse. A blessing that we were not going through it alone and a curse because we couldn't help each other.

Fortunately, we survived this dark period, and we understand each other's needs more now. I recognise when Bill needs his space and he recognises when I need to talk. We intuitively know when we need to be held and we are closer now than ever.

Losing a child is the hardest thing a couple can experience but we have learned to check in with each other on a regular basis. Communication is the key. We share our feelings much more now and we have developed a deep extrasensory skill. We intuitively know how each other feels but most importantly, we know this experience will make us stronger.

Love always shines through.

"No one saves us but ourselves. No one can and no one may. We ourselves must walk the path." Buddha

MY GRIEF BOMB

I go through periods where I feel melancholic and I have an awareness of my tears brimming just under the surface. Sometimes I do not give myself space to let them flow because sometimes it is easier to suppress them. This is when my mind goes into automatic pilot and I allow it to run riot. This is a dangerous place to be because I might drop my grief bomb.

When I hear people discussing everyday mundane stuff like the latest episode of Coronation Street or Brexit or the X factor…….I want to scream, *"REMEMBER MY SON DIED!"* My grief bomb would certainly be a conversation killer.

Bereavement is not a straight line so when I find myself in these periods of sadness, I allow it to happen, knowing it will pass. It is okay to feel like this from time to time but it is important to acknowledge it and allow myself to feel it.

These particularly heavy grief periods are part of the process, like waves and completely normal, but I do believe it is important to become aware of what is going on. When we become fully mindful of these thoughts and feelings and accept them, we can then choose how to react. To not notice what is going on inside, we can become more and more wrapped up in the melancholy energy and before we know it, days, months or possibly years have passed by. Depression is waiting in the wings of melancholy and if we do not see it coming, we can get sucked in.

As a therapist I have many tools in my tool kit to deal with how I am thinking and feeling but if I had not noticed it in the first place, my tools would have just lay there unused.

I will start by sending love to my melancholy. I will allow it to be there and I will welcome it in. I will say, *"Welcome to my body, you can stay as long as you like, I love you."* Melancholy is a message from my body guiding me to notice what is going on and I am listening now. I am listening very carefully and I am grateful for the message. Just noticing it can be enough for the melancholy to dissipate and as I write about it, I can already feel the contrast. I am making peace with each letter as I type.

Now to deal with my grief bomb. I can deactivate it through Tapping Therapy (EFT) but first I need to find out what it consists of. I suspect there is anger because I typed REMEMBER MY SON DIED in shouting capitals. I need to figure out what else is inside before I render the bomb safe. Once I feel the bomb is safe maybe I will do a visualisation and turn it into a chocolate bomb. That is a much safer and much more delicious bomb to carry around or maybe I could take it somewhere safe where the bomb disposal team can blow it up. Even better, I could imagine a cartoon bomb! My imagination is running wild with all sorts of crazy and funny scenarios.

It is okay to not be okay.

Holding onto grief hurts — moving on hurts - letting go hurts. I will endure sadness for it opens my soul.

THE LAKE MEDITATION FOR THE BEREAVED

Adapted from Jon Kabat- Zinn's version

This meditation is normally done in a sitting position. Some people like to record this on their phone so they can listen and follow the guided narration.

Find a comfortable position and place your hands on your lap.

And when you are ready, lower your gaze or allow your eyes to close.

Notice any sounds outside the room.

Notice any sounds within the room.

Become aware of the space around you.

Allow your body to be still, sitting with a sense of dignity, sitting upright with a straight back.

Become aware of your breath as it enters and leaves your body.

Breathing through your nose, notice the physical sensations with each breath - letting the breath be just as it is - without trying to change it in any way - allowing it to flow easily and naturally - with its own rhythm and pace.

As you rest here - allow an image to form in your mind's eye of a lake - a body of water - large or small - held in a receptive basin by the earth itself - water likes to pool in low places - it seeks its own level – being contained.

Even if the lake doesn't come as a visual image - allow the sense of this lake to be there.

As the image of the lake comes into focus – notice its beauty.

Your lake may be deep or shallow - blue or green - muddy or clear.

There may be no wind - the surface may be flat - reflecting trees - sky and clouds.

The wind may come and stir up the waves - causing the reflections to distort and disappear - but then sunlight may sparkle in the ripples - and dance on the waves in a play of shimmering diamonds.

When night comes – it is the moon's turn to dance on the lake - and when the surface is still – the moon is reflected on its surface - along with the outline of trees and shadows.

In winter the lake may freeze over - yet be teeming with movement and life below the surface.

As you rest here - establish this image of a lake in your mind's eye – allowing yourself when you feel ready - to bring the lake inside yourself - so that your being merges with the lake - becoming one with the lake - so that all your energies in this moment are held in awareness with openness and compassion for yourself - in the same way

as the lake's waters are held by the basin of the earth —
you share the same qualities.

Breathing as the lake - feeling its body as your body -
allowing your mind and your heart to be open and
receptive - moment by moment - to reflect whatever
comes near.

Experiencing moments of complete stillness - when
both reflection and water are completely clear - and other
moments perhaps when the surface is disturbed, choppy,
stirred up, reflections and depth lost for the moment.

And through it all as you sit here - simply observing
the play of the various energies of your
own mind and heart - the fleeting thoughts and
feelings - impulses and reactions - which come and go as
ripples and waves - noting their effects.

Noticing the effect of your thoughts and feelings.
Do they disturb the surface and clarity of the mind's
lake?
Do they muddy the waters?
Isn't having a rippling or a wavy surface a part of
being a lake?

Might it be possible to identify not only with the
surface of your lake - but with the entire body of water -
so that you become the stillness below the surface as well
- which at most, experiences only gentle undulations -
even when the surface is choppy.

Below the surface of the lake there is calm — the
deeper into the lake you go, it becomes even more still —

down and down – at the bottom of the lake the water hardly moves – stillness, silence, peace and calm reside at the bottom of your lake – feel these qualities in your body in this moment – allow these qualities to wash through and around you – your lake and body becoming one.

In the same way - in your meditation practice and in your daily life - can you be in touch not only with the changing content and intensity of your thoughts and feelings - but also with the

vast unwavering reservoir of awareness itself - residing below the surface of your mind.

The lake can teach this - remind us of the lake within ourselves.

If you find this image to be of value - you may want to use it from time to time to deepen and

enrich your meditation practice. You might also invite this lake image to empower you and

guide your actions in the world as you move through the unfolding of each day, carrying this vast reservoir of mindfulness within your heart.

Continue to sit here and feel the qualities of the lake– absorbing its energy – feeling resilient – and at peace.

Pause

When you feel ready, bring this meditation to a close by starting to wiggle your fingers and toes. Become aware of the space around you and the room you are in. When you feel ready, open your eyes and notice how you feel.

This meditation can be downloaded FREE from my website.

AN ATTITUDE OF GRATITUDE

Allow yourself to be grateful for what you have and sad for what you have lost.

Before Matthew was diagnosed with cancer, my life was perfect. I describe those days as B.C. before cancer, and these days as A.D. after death!

I feel like a different person now, but grief and loss does change us. We cannot go through this journey and remain the same, but we do have a choice in how we decide to move forward.

I remember a time in my life B.C. when everything was so exciting and full of possibilities and I would wake up each morning and think, "How much better can my life get?" I had worked hard to get myself to this good place and it took years of self-development.

Being a therapist, I loved learning new ways to help my clients and in learning these new ways, it helped me too. Over time I became more confident, and I learned to love and accept the person I had become. (Occasionally my inner child still reminds me there is more work to do, but aren't we all a work in progress?)

Life A.D. of Matthew has been so challenging and I am trying very hard to get back to that exciting, passionate place of infinite possibilities. It just seems wrong to be there now Matthew is not around, but one day I had an 'aha' moment. I was daydreaming about practising my attitude of gratitude again and remembering how great my life was B.C. and then I noticed my thoughts. *"How can you be grateful for your life after what you've been through – you are a heartless person to be grateful for this – you'll never be that happy again – it's all bollocks – get with the real world........."* and my thoughts went on and on and on! I could feel myself slowly sinking back into life A.D. Matthew.

When I became awake to these thoughts, I wondered what Matthew would say if he knew what was going on in my head. My imagination pictured him laughing and saying, *"Come on Mum – get with it – this isn't you – you're the positive one – it's okay to be grateful – I want you to enjoy your life again – stop wasting precious time on negative thinking."*

Well, thank you Matthew, my attitude of gratitude is going to another level and I am going to include you in my affirmations from now on.

Here goes........

"Matthew today – I am grateful for the blue sky."

"Matthew today – I am grateful for the beauty of a deep winter's frost."

"Matthew – I am grateful for this moment."

Life A.D. Matthew, can be whatever I choose it to be!

"Your pain is the breaking of the shell that encloses your understanding." Khalil Gibran

JOURNALING

I have been journaling on and off for a few years and I find it extremely helpful, in fact, that is how my first book 'Letters to Matthew' evolved.

Journaling is a type of writing which invites you to document your thoughts and feelings into a personal book. Unlike a diary where you keep a note of your daily activities, journaling invites you to explore your thoughts and feelings through emotional exploration. It can be effective in helping you clear your mind and establish important connections between your thoughts, feelings and behaviours; it can even reduce the effects of mental illness. This type of reflective writing gives you the opportunity to pause at some point during the day and write down what is really going on inside.

It takes commitment to turn journaling into a positive habit, but it is a healthy way of reflecting on how you are in the moment and how your day has been. When you write down your thoughts and feelings daily in your journal it encourages you to slow down and explore what is going on in your life. It also strengthens the relationship you have with yourself, helping you to understand yourself better.

Journaling also encourages you to focus on any positive experiences you may have had during the day. Anything from someone smiling at you in the queue, to noticing a beautiful flower on your walk to work.

Reflective writing can be an opportunity for you to practise an 'attitude of gratitude'. This was a game changer for me!

Over time journaling can give you clarity and support you towards creating a strong emotional resilience to difficult life events.

We are all going through our own personal journeys but how many of us travel along in automatic pilot? It can be easy to create bad habits when we allow our thoughts and feelings to just carry us along without really noticing how they affect our behaviours and reactions.

Journaling invites you to connect on a much deeper level which connects you to your heart. Your journal book can be your companion, helping you to find clarity and direction in your life. It can be your safe space to document, explore, set intentions, process your thoughts and feelings and guide you on your path to self-discovery.

Use a good old-fashioned pen and an inspiring book to write in and ditch the keyboard. Light a candle and create a sacred space somewhere quiet where you will not be disturbed and allow your words to just flow.

"Fill your paper with the breathings of your heart."
William Wordsworth

Part of grief for me was the worry that I might forget all the pain and anguish, but I can now go back to my journal at any time and read my journal. My journal is a reminder of what I went through, my personal journey. Remembering my darkest days strangely brings me solace but also highlights how far I have come. I recommend everyone starts a journal.

THE SUPERPOWER OF GRIEF

I loved the series 'After Life' by Ricky Gervais. His character Tony found that life without his late wife was meaningless. Feeling like he had nothing to live for, he spent his days being uncomfortably insensitive to his colleagues, the postman, supermarket workers and even children. Wearing his armour of grief, he navigated his way through bereavement being politically incorrect and at times just horrible. It felt awkward to watch but it was also bloody brilliant!

Some days my hubby Bill turns into this Ricky Gervais character. One particular instance was when he'd gone to the local shop to buy some milk, but he was not impressed when he had to join a very long queue at the checkout. With only one checkout operator on, the manager came out and started dancing to the piped music that was being played in the store. Bill was not impressed with this and in front of the queue of smiling customers, Bill informed the manager that he would prefer it if he served behind the counter. The lady behind the checkout said, "Ah, he just wanted to make people smile" but Bill replied that he didn't want to smile, he just wanted his milk! Grief had removed his filters.

I remember Bill telling me that nothing would ever hurt him or impact him as much as the pain of losing our son, Matthew. With this newfound outlook on life, he no longer felt the need to pander to other people or do anything he didn't want to do. I totally understood where he was coming from because I felt the same.

Grief has become my trusty friend and I couldn't imagine my life without it. Don't feel sad for me or think I am a victim because it has bought so much more to my life. It is not something I would have chosen and I'm not saying my life is better now, but it's my new reality and I have made peace with it, plus, it has given me a new superpower called – I Don't Give A Fuck! My superpower has been tamed but Bill is still working on his.

I no longer worry about things in life that I can't control and I feel more relaxed with life in general knowing that change is inevitable and that nothing is permanent. I value time with the people I love and enjoy positive experiences like family time, a cup of coffee with friends, a walk in nature, music, time alone, being present, the smell of rain or freshly cut grass. I now really appreciate what is important in life and I don't spend time thinking about all the other unimportant stuff. What comes with this superpower is a new level of contentment and peace which brings with it a deeper meaning to life.

Has it made me a hard person? Not at all. It doesn't stop me missing Matthew, but it has given me a fresh perspective on life. There's a gift in everything and long may my superpower last!

My hubby Bill on the other hand is still having his Ricky Gervais moments!

Tears water our strength.

.

SPACE CLEARING

When it feels right, it is a good idea to do a space clearing ceremony while you are grieving. It helps to have a good flow of clear, high vibrational energy in your home for your own health and well-being. This is something you can control.

Space clearing is a ceremony that can be done to clear and refresh the energies that may have become imprinted in your home over time.

The vibration of whatever happens in a room or home is absorbed into the furniture, the floors, the walls, the ceiling, objects, animals, plants, and people. Emotions, moods, and atmospheres all get deeply imprinted and this can have an on-going influence whether you are consciously aware of it or not.

Have you ever walked into a room after there has been an argument? Your expanded senses can feel and measure the residual energies where the air is so thick you could '*cut it with a knife*'. This energy is easy to feel because it so heavy but there are other more subtle energies around that are more difficult to pick up.

The benefits of space clearing your home after a loss are many. It helps to clear the emotional residue which builds up over time and it creates a positive space helping you to move forward. This will help improve sleep and your general well-being. It also creates an atmosphere of calm and space to make a new start. Your space will feel bigger and brighter helping you to move in the right direction emotionally.

How to do a space clearing ceremony.
Ideally do this when you are on your own and at a time when you will not be disturbed.

Before starting any energetic space clearing you need to de-clutter and physically clean your home first. Open all the windows and doorways. Set your intention to cleanse and energise the area to create a high vibrational atmosphere. You could write down your positive intentions or say them out loud.
For example:
"As I clear this space, I call ask for protection and invite love, light, and peace to fill this space. May the energy flowing through here be for my highest good. I open this space to divine love."

Ask the angels, guides, or other high vibrational beings to help you, if this feels right for you.

Light a white tea candle in each area you are working in.
Using incense, walk into each area and allow the incense smoke to drift into every corner and doorway. Visualise a bright light in each area as you go.

If you prefer to not use incense you can use bells, ting shas, cymbals, drums and singing bowls for space clearing. If you use these instruments, it is important to sound them especially in the corners, doorways and the centre of the area. The vibration of the sound will resonate out like ripples on a pond and transmute any heavy energy into high vibrational energy.

To help keep this space cleared you can use crystals. Amethyst crystal is an extremely powerful and protective crystal prized for its beauty, healing, and spiritual properties but there are many different crystals you may choose to suit your own individual needs. You can leave them out like ornaments or create a crystal grid effect.

Burning essential oils is a very natural and enjoyable way of filling your space with a beautiful aroma. Pure 100% essential oils have the highest frequency of any measured natural substance and the essence of this will help your space stay fresher for longer.

Place lavender plants outside by your front and back doors. Lavender is a plant spirit medicine that exudes the qualities of love, peace, and calm. It is a very protective and nurturing plant which will infuse your space with the essence of its qualities.

Wouldn't your loved ones appreciate a high vibrational space helping them to find peace too?

If you invite angels, guides, or other high vibrational beings in to help, thank them for their help when you have finished space clearing and send them your love.

When to do a space clearing ceremony.

As you move through the bereavement process you will have good days and bad days. Some days you may not want to get out of bed and other days you may feel more productive. You will know when it feels right for you.

A space clearing ceremony is good to do anytime but particularly when moving into a new home or workspace to clear out any predecessor's energy. Your home or place of work may have energetic remains from all the previous people that were there and depending on the age of the place, this could be from decades or even centuries.

When selling your house so it welcomes a new buyer (also renting).

After illness to create a healthy environment.

After negative visitors (especially energy vampires!)

After an argument or any emotional upset.

Before the birth of a child to create a welcoming space.

After a major negative life changing event.

I recommend this space clearing ceremony is performed at least once a year or sooner if you experience a major life changing event.

Sometimes we're tested - not to show our weaknesses but to discover our strengths.

MINDFULNESS & GRIEF

Mindfulness is a much researched, evidence based, self-help tool which has become extremely popular over the last few years. I am naturally interested in health and well-being, so I became a mindfulness teacher in 2018.

There are two forms of mindfulness, informal and formal.

1) Informal mindfulness encourages you to live your life in a mindful way. Being in the moment as much as possible.

2) Formal mindfulness is the daily practice of meditation.

(There are FREE mindfulness meditations on my website www.louisebates.co.uk)

I find mindfulness very helpful now but in the early days of my grief experience, mindfulness was not something I could have considered. Mindfulness encourages us to be in the moment but when your moment is full of raw grief and sadness, being in the moment is not the best place to be. Distractions work better during this time i.e. television, radio or being around others may be more beneficial in the early stages. Over time as you grow around your grief, mindfulness can potentially enhance your mental health and well-being supporting you to keep moving in the right direction.

Mindfulness has been around for centuries and there are many forms including, guided meditations, walking meditations, tai chi, mantras and many more.

The Hindus and Buddhists were practising meditation over 2,500 years ago. Modern mindfulness draws upon these traditions. The mindfulness movement today takes elements from these different forms of meditation and simplifies the practice. There are no belief systems required to practise mindfulness.

The connection between Buddhism and mindfulness:
- Buddhism concentrates on stilling the mind and being in the present moment as part of their teachings toward awakening and enlightenment.
- Mindfulness shares the importance of stilling the mind and being in the present moment but being detached to any outcomes.

Mindfulness is a mental process achieved by focusing your awareness on the present moment. Yesterday has gone, tomorrow has not arrived and all that is real is this present moment.

Mindfulness practice involves bringing your attention to the here and now and noticing each breath as it flows in and out of your body. It uses the breath as an anchor to keep bringing yourself into the present moment. It is about acknowledging, observing and accepting what is going on inside your mind and body, it is not about changing what's there.

Mindfulness also includes seven attitudes to practice alongside formal and informal meditations.

Seven attitudes of mindfulness:

Non-judging: It is human nature to judge and compare yourself to others, but mindfulness encourages you to notice and have an awareness of when you do this. When you practise non-judging, it is helpful to notice the habit of labelling your experiences as good or bad, etc. It is just as important to become aware of how you judge yourself too. The relationship you have with yourself is the most important relationship you will ever have. When you practise mindfulness, you become more aware of the self-talk and self-criticism that goes on. When you become aware of this, you can learn to be kinder and to practice self-compassion. This will then radiate out and create subtle changes in the world around you.

Patience: Jon Kabat-Zinn (an American professor emeritus of medicine and the creator of the Stress Reduction Clinic and the Center for Mindfulness) explains that patience is *"the soil in which you will be cultivating your ability to calm your mind and relax your body, to concentrate and to see more clearly."* Practising patience relieves feelings of frustration, restlessness and anger. You can practice patience while standing in a queue and be grateful for that moment. You can practice patience while being stuck in a traffic jam and feel grateful for the time it allows for you to really notice your surroundings. When you feel you are becoming impatient for whatever reason, that is an invitation to be mindfully patient.

Beginner's mind: The beginners mind encourages you to experience each day as if you were experiencing each one for the first time, i.e. like seeing the world through a new lens. Do you take things for granted and forget to notice the beauty in everyday things such as, the walk to work, a cup of coffee, a simple flower, etc. Looking at life with fresh eyes from one moment to the next, helps you to see things from different perspectives. A beginner's mind is an open mind and life can be more enjoyable from this viewpoint.

Trust: Trust starts with yourself. When you trust yourself first, you are more open to trusting others. We already trust that the breath comes in and the breath goes out and that each system in our body works without any conscious effort. We trust the sun will rise each morning and set each day. The tide will come in and out. Transfer this trust to other aspects of your life. Mindfulness takes time to practice but you can choose to trust that all is well and as it should be.

Non-striving: We live in a fast paced, material world and generally people find it hard to keep up. Non-striving invites us to - just be and to slow down and smell the coffee. Life is not a race or competition. Non-striving encourages us to be happy with what we have and where we are in this moment. Life is for each moment to count without the need for more money, the summer holiday, the bigger house, the better car, retirement, etc. Non-striving takes away the pressure and unease that comes from thoughts and feelings like *"I will be happy when......"* Allow yourself to feel content even if it is for a fleeting moment. You don't have to wait for things to get easier because life will always be complicated.

Acceptance: This attitude allows you to accept the thoughts, feelings and sensations that show up inside. Instead of resisting or trying to get rid of them, you can be the observer and just notice them. This means you do not have to do any work, just be with whatever comes up. Acceptance is hard when you are grieving but allow yourself small moments. No judging, striving, or trying to change anything. Just pure acceptance.

Letting go: It is easy for your thoughts to be consumed by the past and to dwell on situations that have happened or to worry about the future and what might happen. Mindfulness nurtures you to be in the present moment which allows the mind to stop taking you back into the past or into the future and in effect it allows you to let go of any negative thoughts or feelings. Letting go seems impossible when you have lost a loved one but you are not letting go of your loved one; you are letting go of whatever it is that doesn't serve you.

The thoughts you hold onto that do not serve you, are only thoughts and thoughts are not real. With practice, mindfulness teaches you to just notice these thoughts with a detached view. I like to think of my thoughts as trains passing through a train station - I just watch them come and go. I can choose which train I want to get on and that is my way of dealing with any unpleasant or intrusive thoughts. Choose your thoughts wisely.

It does not take long for our brains to start creating a new pattern of thinking through neuroplasticity. The brain has an ever-changing potential as it develops new neural pathways depending on whatever habits we get into. Our mindset is just another habit, a way of thinking.

To create new neural pathways, you need to shift your focus and over time, the more you practice mindfulness, the stronger these pathways will become.

Practicing the seven attitudes of mindfulness along with self-compassion and gratitude are powerful ways to kick start building these new pathways in your brain.

With time, it has been proved, we can literally rewire the neural pathways that control our emotions, thoughts, and reactions. This means we can create new neural pathways in our brain that lead us naturally to compassion, gratitude, and joy. We have the ability to reprogramme our brain, but it requires a conscious effort.

Three easy daily mindfulness practices:
1. Involve your five senses to fully experience your morning shower. Notice the temperature of the water, the aroma of the shampoo and body wash, the bubbles on your hair and body, how the shower makes you feel – revitalised – awake.

2. Eat your meals mindfully. Eat slowly, tasting every morsel. Notice the texture of the food as well as the taste. Notice the temperature. Eat without any distractions. Turn off the TV, radio and most importantly, turn off your mobile phone. Stop eating when you feel full.

3. Practice mindfulness meditations.

The mind and body are connected, and mindfulness is not just about what is going on in the mind. It is about what is going on in the body as well. When you allow yourself to fully tune into what sensations are happening within the physical body you develop a deeper sense of awareness. It is important to passively observe the body and its actions without thinking in terms of good or bad, attractive, or unattractive. The goal is to accept yourself in the process with a non-judgmental awareness which creates greater self-acceptance.

Tai chi and yoga are good examples of how we can tune into ourselves mindfully through movement, but a slow walk around the garden or even in your lounge can be done mindfully.

Practising mindfulness takes years to master but even more so during a bereavement. Be gentle with yourself and just dip your toe in. Appreciate that mindfulness can support you in processing your grief and loss experience, but you do not need to become an expert in it.

Benefits of mindfulness during bereavement:

Improves self-awareness / body awareness:

When you have a deeper understanding of yourself, you can observe yourself as a unique and separate being. You are then empowered to make changes and build on your areas of strength as well as identify areas where you would like to make improvements.

Decreases stress / anxiety:

Chronic stress and anxiety disrupts nearly every system in the body and long-term exposure can lead to serious health issues. Over time, stress has the potential to rewire the brain, leaving you more vulnerable to depression and anxiety. Practicing mindfulness helps to restore the body to a better state so improving physical and mental wellbeing.

Strengthens resilience / improves mental health:
Mindfulness creates a new awareness that helps you build a different relationship between your thoughts and feelings. This helps you to move forward in your life in a much more positive way.

Improves confidence / Self-esteem:
Through mindfulness, any personal struggles can be acknowledged and accepted. The seven mindfulness attitudes can then be incorporated to nurture self-compassion improving how you view yourself.

Improves physical health / Strengthens immune system:
Stress can suppress the immune system, raise blood pressure, increase the risk of heart attack and stroke, contribute to infertility, and speed up the ageing process. Practicing mindfulness helps to restore the body's equilibrium which over time, improves physical health.

Mindfulness can potentially support the bereaved with:
- Stress reduction
- Greater resilience
- Improved concentration
- Improved health and wellbeing
- Ability to have better sleep

"You only lose what you cling to." Buddha

GUIDED MEDITATION

Mindfulness is a powerful skill to master but guided meditations may be more beneficial than mindfulness in the early stages of grief.

Guided meditations take you on a journey and encourage you to use your imagination. The music and narration on these meditations creates beautiful landscapes for your mind to walk through or spend time in.

When your mind is focusing on being in a beautiful landscape, beach, or mountain for example, it cannot differentiate between reality or what it is imagining or thinking. While you focus your full attention on the guided meditation your mind believes you are there, and it releases the feel-good hormones endorphins which can change how you feel.

Guided meditations will give you temporary relief from your sadness, and this has the potential to help you move forward.

This could be another small nudge in the right direction preventing you from becoming stuck in your grief.

I have a variety of guided meditations on my website which can be downloaded for FREE.

"Peace comes from within. Do not seek it without." Buddha

CONSCIOUS GRIEVING

The human emotion of grief is one of the most difficult experiences we encounter and it cannot be side tracked, it must be felt. The early weeks, months and years of grief can be brutal and for some it can be never-ending.

The pain of grief and loss is proof that we loved a very special person and the love we have for that person when they're gone, has nowhere to go. Conscious grieving is about navigating the grief journey from a mindful perspective. (Caution! This may not be good advice for someone who is newly bereaved or maybe it will).

Over time the waves of grief come further and further apart and you get a chance to catch your breath. Everyone experiences grief differently and there is no time limit to when this happens. When you get a space in between the waves you can choose to view your loss not as some tragic, random, meaningless life event, but as an opportunity to explore the bigger picture. This is when conscious grieving can become helpful.

Conscious grieving is an invitation to fully participate into the process and observe your thoughts and feelings. This could potentially help you develop an understanding that you do have a choice whether to tune into the pain and loss of your loved one, or tune into the love you still have for them. Conscious grieving unblocks a different perspective which cultivates a deeper self-awareness. This can then lead on to a healthy connection with the energy of your loved one.

I was overwhelmed with sadness recently by a song on the radio. It had sentimental meaning and a connection to Matthew and in that moment, I could have broken down and cried. The song had triggered me. I could have allowed myself to get dragged down into the grief vortex, but I took a moment and consciously thought about how this song had affected me. I could feel the pain of loss in my solar plexus, a tension across my chest, the tears pooling in my eyes and the sadness, such tremendous sadness in my whole body. Instead of breaking down, I put both my hands on my heart, I took in a deep breath, and I spoke gently to the sadness in my body. *"I give you permission to be here, you can stay as long as you like, I love you, thank you."* I felt the love I had for Matthew deep inside and focused on this. Within a few moments, the sadness lifted and in my mind's eye I could see Matthew smiling and looking happy.

I genuinely believe that when we make peace with our grief and loss moments, this sends peace to our loved ones too.

I hope this inspires you to become more mindful of your own grieving process wherever you are in your journey. Observe your thoughts and feelings and give them permission to be there. These thoughts and feelings are your body's inner guidance system communicating with you. Send love to them. Talk to them. Do not resist them or push them down. Be gentle with yourself and respect the grieving process.

This ongoing reflection and inner work can help you move forward in a more positive way.

There is no cure for grief. Remember it can only be acknowledged, absorbed, carried, experienced, loved and cared for.

In the stillness, I am here.

I needed to experience frustration to learn patience.
I needed to experience rejection to learn acceptance.
I needed to experience suffering to learn compassion and empathy.
I needed to experience disappointment to learn appreciation.
I needed to experience hurt to learn forgiveness.
I needed to experience doubt to learn trust.
I needed to experience loss to understand grief.
I am still a work in progress and that's okay!

SLEEPLESS NIGHTS

Most grievers experience sleepless nights. It may seem like grief comes more to the surface at night and it feels worse, but the stillness during the hours of darkness amplifies your thoughts and emotions.

Losing a spouse/partner is noticeably a big factor in experiencing sleepless nights. This form of loss may be the most likely to cause insomnia and sleep loss. Theories suggest having to adjust to a new sleeping arrangement (no longer sharing a bed) as one of the top reasons in this scenario.

Listening to a relaxation audio is very soothing, especially at bedtime or during those nights where you just cannot sleep. Using headphones really helped me to tune in and filter out any distractions. There are various free meditation apps or guided meditations you can access that can be very useful at night when your mind goes into overdrive. This helps you to focus your attention on something relaxing which helps to feel more calm and more peaceful. You are more likely to fall asleep in this state. Alternatively, find an uplifting, inspiring podcast or anything that interests you, maybe gardening or cooking or fishing, whatever works for you. There are some fab grief podcasts that helped me. There are thousands of free podcasts out there which will help you to switch off and relax.

I also find focusing my attention on certain aspects of being in bed help me to get to sleep. For example, I notice how comfortable my bed is - how lovely the sheets feel against my skin - how warm and cosy I feel – how soft my pillows are – how safe I feel – I notice the stillness – the peacefulness – there is nothing to do but relax. I keep repeating these thoughts in my mind until I eventually fall asleep. Sometimes when I wake in the middle of the night, I follow this process again.

Whether you choose to follow a meditation app, or practice mindfulness or count sheep, having lots of different resources to go to is much better than lying there for hours getting upset by your thoughts and not being able to sleep. Even being able to relax, helps your body cope with what is going on.

Losing sleep is a normal thing that everyone goes through from time to time, especially in times of distress or sadness, but that does not diminish the terrible impact it can have on your body. Getting less than seven hours sleep at night could increase the likelihood of health conditions such as, diabetes, heart conditions, obesity, or anxiety. In some cases, chronic insomnia may increase the possibility of certain cancers due to the disruption of the circadian rhythm and changes to the immune system and hormones. Some people turn to sleeping pills which can be prescribed as a stepping-stone to getting through a difficult period, but it is best to find a strategy that works for you. Talk to your doctor to discuss this further.

Being the best you can be may never be enough, but be your best anyway.

SMILE WHEN YOU FEEL SAD

Why would you want to smile when you feel sad?

There may come a time where you start to feel stuck in your grief. Maybe you have been grieving for years and you find it impossible to do anything about it. Long term grief hardwires you to be trapped and it can seem impossible to be any other way. The longer you experience the grieving process the stronger and better you get at being that way.

Your thoughts create a pattern of thinking and over time repetitive thoughts create a mindset. Your mind becomes set on thinking in a particular way. Your thoughts then control your feelings and over time it becomes your natural default setting. If you are constantly thinking repetitive sad thoughts, you will constantly feel sad. In the same way that people with depression get stuck, you can find yourself stuck in grief.

Neuroplasticity:
The neurons in your brain get used to firing in a certain direction and over time the more you think the same way the stronger these connections become. Neurons are information messengers. They use electrical impulses and chemical signals to transmit information

between different areas of the brain, and between the brain and the rest of the nervous system. Your brain will constantly rewire itself to suit the information that you feed it. For example, if you constantly complain, gossip, find excuses, feel sad, it will make it much easier to find things to be upset about regardless of what is going on around you. Likewise, if you constantly search for opportunities, abundance, love, and things to be grateful for, it will make it much easier to find a reflection of those things around you. It takes practice, but over time, it is possible to reshape your reality.

Have you become an expert in grief? Maybe you have practiced it for years, day after day, month after month, year after year. Maybe you have become such an expert you could have a certificate in how to grieve or maybe even a degree! You could potentially teach others how to grieve because you are so good at it. Maybe you have been doing it for so long it has become your comfort zone. Maybe you do not know who you would be without it.

I noticed my thoughts were taking me down this path. I was good at practising the same remunerating thoughts, but I became aware of what this was creating in my mind. I was a mindfulness teacher and I knew how easy it was for my mind to go into automatic pilot mind and be unconsciously swept along towards a negative mindset. As a therapist I was an expert at supporting and helping others, but it was now time to use my expertise on me. I could utilize my training. I had tools in my therapist tool kit just waiting to be used but if I had not noticed what was happening, those tools would have laid idle. One of those tools was to practice smiling!

I practice smiling a lot (which makes me sound completely bonkers, and I probably am) but it does help. The science behind this has been proved that when we smile, tiny muscles at the side of our mouth send messages to the brain that say we are smiling. The brain then sends out the endorphins (the body's feel-good hormones) which flood the body changing your biology and chemistry. This makes you feel good which then improves your mood.

Yes, it is false positivity, but you are not denying your sadness or ignoring the grieving process, you are just practising smiling. Fake it till you make it!

If you practice this on and off – day after day, you will start to notice a difference. It's not the cure for grief because there is no cure, but it helps you to put one foot in front of the other and move forward in a more positive way.

Living your best life is the greatest way to honour your loved one.

PHYSICAL SYMPTOMS OF GRIEF

When you are grieving, your body holds all the love you have for that person, but the love has nowhere to go. It is that lump in your throat. That pain in your chest that restricts you from breathing properly. It is that knot in your stomach that will not go away. It is those tears that fall from your eyes. It is your own personal experience which can change from one moment to the next. By recognising and allowing your body to feel this, you can start to process it. Give yourself permission to feel what you feel and acknowledge and accept every physical sensation. What we resist, persists.

The strong emotions that are part and parcel of grief create an incredibly stressful internal environment which can be like battery acid inside the body.

At first grief can feel like an intense physical pain. It can bring you to your knees and take your breath away and people have been known to die of a broken heart. This is known as broken heart syndrome, a condition that mimics a heart attack with symptoms such as chest pain and shortness of breath. The medical term for this is Takotsubo cardiomyopathy.

The heartbreak of grief can also increase blood pressure and the risk of blood clots.

Anxiety can increase and this can affect your breathing. It can feel like you have a tight band across your chest. Panic attacks can follow this.

Grief can create overwhelming tiredness, exhaustion and restlessness, yet you may find it impossible to relax.

Grief can produce a lot of unexplained aches and pains including increased headaches.

Grief increases inflammation, which can worsen any health problems you may already have or cause new ones.

Grief compromises the immune system, leaving you depleted and vulnerable to infection.

Grief makes it hard to think straight or make decisions and it has been described as, living in a fog.

Grief affects your appetite. With the disruption to your normal eating habit or routine it can cause temporary problems with your digestive system, such as constipation, diarrhea, stomach pain or feeling nauseated. This can lead to weight loss. For some, eating can bring comfort and this can lead to weight gain.

People sometimes complain of a lump in the throat. This is caused by the combination of anxiety, tension and sadness being held in the throat area. There is no actual lump, but it is always a good idea to get yourself checked out to put your mind at ease.

Grief can trigger early onset dementia.

Grief is not a mental disorder, but it can easily turn into one.

If you are worried about any symptoms, talk to your doctor. You may just need reassurance that you are okay and it will put your mind at rest.

Your physical body has an inner guidance system which sends messages to you about the state it is in. When you tune into your body and acknowledge what you feel, you can start to process your grief experience.

Having a rough day?
Put your hand on your heart and feel it.
That's life - so don't give up.

GRIEF EXERCISE

Caution! This exercise may not be helpful if you are in the early stages of grief - or for some people maybe it is. Everyone is different.

A few months after my son Matthew died this exercise proved to be helpful to me. It transformed those emotions that were unexpectedly triggered by a song on the radio, or some other sentimental moment. You know, those moments that catch you off guard. This exercise really works too. It helps to transcend the heavy emotions, leaving a warm glow inside which connects you to your loved one.

I suggest you read through the exercise first and see if it feels suitable for you.

Exercise:
When you experience a wave of grief notice the feelings, emotions and sensations inside.
Place both your hands on your heart and take three deep long breaths in and out.
Keep your hands on your heart and notice where in your body you feel the wave of grief. Observe the wave and notice if it moves from one place to another, for

example, from your chest to your tummy or is it everywhere?

Do not label the feeling, for example, sadness, pain, sorrow, heartache, anger, etc. Just notice the sensation. Your mind will unconsciously start looking for references to remember other times when you felt this feeling or sensation. The mind wants to make sense of this information and by connecting with a similar feeling or sensation it gives it more power. Do not allow your mind to take over. Keep yourself in the present moment. Notice your breath and tune into your feelings. Really connect to your body.

Where is the feeling?

Is it in your chest, your tummy or somewhere else?

How intense is the feeling on a scale of one to ten, with ten being the most intense?

Notice how it feels, observe it, but do not give the sensation a label.

Can you visualise the feeling inside?

Does it have a colour?

If it feels right for you, talk to the feeling inside, for example, *"I allow and acknowledge this feeling inside, I love you, you can stay as long as you like, thank you."*

Visualise pure unconditional love pouring from your heart and washing through you and notice what happens, be patient. The feeling may be uncomfortable but allow it to feel safe inside as you send it love. Just notice it, allow it to be there. Really notice it. Sit with it. Accept it. Allow it to feel welcome. Offer a virtual hug to this feeling. Welcome it in like a small child and then send it love, send it love, send it love.

Know that this feeling inside is a link to your loved one. The pain of grief is proof you loved.

You may find, after a while, the feeling may shift and move or completely transcend.

You may get an insight, an uplifting message or an inner knowing that all is well. Sometimes we just need to feel it and not fight or resist it.

Is the feeling still there?

If it is, ask yourself, "Do you want to let it go?"

If the answer is yes, give yourself permission to let it go.

Place both your hands on your heart, close your eyes and say, *"I give myself permission to let go of this feeling"*.

Notice any resistance and send it love, send it love, send it love.

If the answer is no - that is fine too. Allow the feeling to be there. Give it permission to be there. It can stay as long as you want it to. Send it love, send it love, send it love.

This exercise is not about releasing all the grief because that would be impossible, but it gives you deep insights into what is going on inside and helps you to understand how you are processing your experience. It invites you to take some control into how you are grieving.

"Grief can be the garden of compassion. If you keep your heart open through everything, your pain can become your greatest ally in your eyes search for love and wisdom." Rumi

THE FALLOUT OF GRIEF

Grief and the emotions felt due to a loss, can be incredibly hard to cope with for both the bereaved and for those who are trying to be supportive. Hopefully, with mutual respect and patience, relationships can withstand the pain of loss and in some cases may grow even stronger.

Unfortunately, after losing a loved one, relationships do sometimes break down. The rawness of grief generates many overwhelming emotions and that can make it difficult to think straight. When people are in this vortex of high emotions they may behave differently or say things they would not ordinarily say. Also, the griever may be picking up on a thoughtless comment or get confused by another person's well-meaning act of kindness. Anything can be a trigger when you are on your knees and your world is crashing down around you.

When a loved one dies, there is nothing anyone can do or say to take away the pain inside. Anger is part of grief and it can be easy to lash out at others. Typically, it is the people we love that get hurt the most. They are probably grieving too and just coping the best they can to survive each day. Grievers close to the deceased will be falling apart and the intense painful emotions are like a time bomb waiting to go off. It doesn't take much for people to fall out.

How often do you hear about people falling out over the funeral arrangements or not being left something they believe they are entitled to? It is so sad, and some relationships never recover from this fallout. When a loved one dies those closest to the deceased will feel the most intense emotions, but this is not a free ticket to control or claim their loved one's personal effects. Even if there is a will, this does not offer protection from the fallout of grief. There can be disagreements even years later.

The pain of loss does strange things to people but when you have lost someone you love dearly, the fear of losing anything else is unbearable. This could be anything that connects you, such as a personal effect, or some sentimental item you want to hang on to with all your might. This does not make you a bad person, it just shows how desperate you are to hold onto anything that comforts you and makes you feel closer to the person who died. You need that connection. Your loss is enormous and hard to comprehend and the thought of losing anything else is too much. It is like holding onto some part of the shipwreck to stay afloat. Letting go is a hard part of the grieving process.

Letting go of your loved one's possessions.
Whether it is their clothes, their possessions, or anything else, it will not make the pain any less by holding onto these things. Their material things are just 'things'. You will always have their memories which are the gifts they have left behind for you to keep. The memories you

hold in your heart are the greatest gifts. Our loved one's material things are like the broken parts of a shipwreck but in reality, they are just a distraction. It is good to have one or two items for sentimental connections but learn to let go of anything else. Do it in your time and when it feels right for you.

You may not want to mend the broken relationships and maybe that is for the best, but send them loving thoughts. They were connected to the deceased too and you have no idea how they processed their grief. Send them love, send them love, send them love.

Sometimes the worst place to be is inside your own head!

REASON, SEASON, OR LIFETIME

Reason

People come into your life for a reason, a season, or a lifetime.

When you figure out which one it is, you will know what to do for each person.

When someone is in your life for a reason, it is usually to meet a need you have expressed.

They have come to assist you through a difficulty, to provide you with guidance and support, to aid you physically, emotionally, or spiritually.

They may seem like a godsend, and they are.

They are there for the reason you need them to be.

Then, without any wrongdoing on your part or at an inconvenient time, this person will say or do something to bring the relationship to an end.

Sometimes they die. Sometimes they walk away. Sometimes they act up and force you to take a stand.

What we must realise is that our need has been met, our desire fulfilled; their work is done.

The prayer you sent up has been answered and now it is time to move forward.

Season

Some people come into your life for a season, because your turn has come to share, grow, or learn.

They bring you an experience of peace or make you laugh.

They may teach you something you have never done.

They usually give you an unbelievable amount of joy.

Believe it. It is real. But only for a season.

Lifetime

Lifetime relationships teach you lifetime lessons, things you must build upon in order to have a solid emotional foundation.

Your job is to accept the lesson, love the person and put what you have learned to use in all other relationships and areas of your life.

Author unknown

HOLDING THE HAND OF A LOVED ONE AS THEY DIE

Not everyone can be by the side of a loved one as they pass away. Sometimes a loved one may pass before you have a chance to get to them, or they could die suddenly or tragically without warning. Nothing can prepare you for this. During covid some people had to say goodbye over an iPad or phone which to me was completely inhumane.

It really is a privilege to be able to hold the hand of a loved one as they transition out of this world. It is traumatic and emotional, and you have no control when their body has had enough and decides to shut down. The moment they take their last breath is a special moment between two worlds and you may feel surrounded by an incredible sacredness.

Their last breath takes your breath away.

What follows is different for everyone and it is hard to know how to prepare yourself for this moment.

They're gone!

Disbelief and overwhelming emotions will follow but there are things you can do to help prepare for this moment. If your loved one dies in a care home, hospital or hospice surrounded by medical staff, they will take control and guide you. If your loved one dies peacefully at home surrounded by family, you may feel unsure what to do at first. We are not qualified to deal with death, and it is normal to feel unprepared and panic. Emotions will be all over the place and it will be hard to think straight.

If you can, this is a good time to really feel present in the moment. Carry on holding their hand, connect to the stillness, observe your loved one while they are still warm, caress their hair, kiss them, tell them you will always love them – this moment can never be repeated. This is your opportunity to tell them everything. Maybe even make yourself a cup of tea and then just sit with them, be present with them. Can you feel other energies in the room? Really connect to the sacredness of this moment. Taking this time out to be with your loved one gives you a chance to pause and experience your loved one's transition. Sending them on their way peacefully may be hard when all you want to do is not let them go.........let them go. There is plenty of time to fall to pieces, to feel broken, to grieve, so try not to miss the specialness of this moment. You'll never get this time back again.

After ten or fifteen minutes, you can call who you need to call and do what you need to do.

This is great advice I wish someone had told me before my son Matthew died. We get birth training and prepare to bring new life into this world, but nothing prepares us for when a loved ones dies.

Being present at the moment a loved one dies is a very intimate and private act. If you can stay calm and keep the energy in the room serene, it will allow your loved one to feel more peaceful and maybe this will help them to transition in the most beautiful way. You will both feel the benefit.

"I am not this hair, I am not this skin, I am the soul that lives within." Rumi

TEARS FOR PRAYERS

You know I feel your sorrow, you know I feel your pain.

You fear that you have lost me, and we will never meet again.

Maybe you think prayers went unheard.

Maybe you've lost your faith

But there is a bigger picture, and your faith is what it takes.

Those with whom we've walked in love, we will see again.

This is God's divine promise see, there really is no end.

Don't grieve for me for you must know, I'm in a bright new dimension.

Where beauty fills each joyous moment way beyond your comprehension.

So rest in peace dear loved one, change your tears to prayers.

Know that every one you say for me, sends me peace beyond compare.

For in heaven time is nothing, you'll know one day for sure.

And there's nothing that will keep me, from holding you once more.

© Patricia Mary Finn - Printed with permission

SUPPORT YOURSELF WHILE GRIEVING

- When it feels right for you, talk to people about the person who has died and keep your memories alive.
- Talk to people about your thoughts and how you feel.
- Look after yourself by eating properly.
- When you need space to be alone - be alone.
- It may be difficult to sleep but just resting is beneficial.
- Scream and shout if you want to.
- Drink plenty of water, tears might dehydrate you.
- Give yourself time and permission to feel what you feel.
- Seek help and support if you feel you need it.
- Book yourself a relaxing massage.
- Do not be afraid to tell people what you need.
- Write a letter to your loved one. Light a candle and hold a personal item of your loved one like a watch or a photograph and create a calm loving atmosphere; then start writing. Explain how you feel and share your thoughts. No one else needs to see this letter. It is only for you and your loved one.

- Listen to music.
- Keep breathing. Deep breaths are so healing to our heart, our minds, and our emotions.
- Watch comedies
- If you have no-one to talk to, contact me.

People may say the following phrases and they may help, or they may not. Nothing anyone says will make you feel better. Remember these people are doing their best and at least be grateful that they have acknowledged your grief.

- I am sorry for your loss.
- I wish I had the right words but know I care.
- I do not know how you feel but I am here to help in any way.
- You and your loved one will be in my thoughts and prayers.
- My favourite memory of your loved one is…
- He/she was a wonderful person.

Sometimes people turn the conversation on themselves because they do not know how to engage with you. Phrases like, 'my dad died last year', or 'I know how you feel', cancels out your feelings and it is important you feel validated. Not everyone will get it right and this is probably the best they can do. Here are some unhelpful phrases you may hear:

At least they had a good life.
It doesn't matter how good their life was, it does not stop the pain of grief.

They are in a better place now.
A better place for who?

They are not suffering any more.
This may be true, but grief is about you, not the person who died.

I know how you feel.
No, you don't! Grief is as individual as a fingerprint. No one will understand how you feel.

My Dad died of cancer.
And how is this helpful? (Remember this person is just trying to engage on some level.)

It was their time.
No, it wasn't! But if it was their time, the grief still needs validating.

There's always a reason.
What was the reason?

They had a good innings.
This old chestnut always comes out when an elderly person dies but this cliché is as useless as a chocolate tea pot.

These unhelpful phrases kill the conversation making it difficult for the griever to express themselves. It is important to understand that not everyone has experienced grief and loss, and they may not know what else to say. These clumsy cliché phrases are commonly used so they think they are being helpful. Their intentions are good and at least they have acknowledged your grief which is important. You can be grateful for that!

Love and support can come in many ways. (How you can help others who are grieving.)

- Bake a cake or prepare a hot meal.
- Take some groceries around. Food shopping can be so hard for the griever.
- Write them a letter and share your favourite memories of the deceased person.
- Offer to do their shopping or look after the children or take their dog for a walk.
- People who have been bereaved may want to talk about the person who has died. One of the most helpful things you can do is simply listen and give them time and space to grieve. Encourage the person to talk and then really listen to them.
- Contact the person at difficult times especially anniversaries and birthdays.
- Be empathetic. Empathy is an intuitive connection to the feelings and emotions of other people.
- Send them a text to say you are thinking about them.
- Ask if it is okay to keep checking in on them.
- Mention the name of the deceased person. Their name hasn't died, and it is comforting to hear their name being mentioned.

We can be going along minding our own business and everything seems to be okay. Then, out of nowhere, grief hits full force. This is not a setback. It is simply part of the grieving process.

GETTING UNSTUCK

There is no end to grief, just a beginning, a middle and the rest of your life.

It may feel more comfortable for you to sit with your deep sadness and do nothing to move out of the grief vortex and that is okay. It takes effort to be any other way and grief cannot be rushed, but it can be loosened! You are not disrespecting your loved one or the grieving process by moving forward. Moving forward can be just taking one small step at a time. Moving forward can be just forcing yourself to open your eyes first thing in the morning. Moving forward can be taking deep breaths in and out. Moving forward can be just taking a shower. Moving forward doesn't have to be massive occurrences. You just need to be pointing in the right direction.

Feeling sad every time you think about your loss is not being stuck. Even years later you can be bought to your knees by a sentimental song on the radio, or a special anniversary, or just randomly for no reason other than you just miss that person. Grief can highjack you at any time now or in the future. This is not being stuck.

Grief is part of human suffering, but it is not a mental illness, although it can very easily become one. The worst part about grief is getting stuck, and this can happen whatever type of grief you experience. Grief and depression can look similar but there are some key differences.

Grief

Early grief is raw and constant. Dark thoughts, anguish, pain, and deep sadness is normal. As the rawness of grief ebbs and wanes you will start to notice it comes in waves. Some waves will feel like tsunamis which will bring you to your knees and some waves will be a gentle swell and make you sob. Where grief and depression differ is that grief occurs in waves when you are triggered by thoughts or reminders of your loss. Other negative emotions may be present, but the rawness of grief tends to decrease over time as you grow around it. You will learn to smile and laugh again but you will feel the ache still there deep down. The ache of grief will follow you around like a shadow. After a while and it's different for everyone, you will feel okay in certain situations, but triggers like anniversaries etc. even decades later may cause the intense feelings to resurface.

Depression

Depression on the other hand, tends to be more persistent. Symptoms of depression include feeling unhappy, hopeless, suicidal, with low self-esteem and finding no pleasure in things you usually enjoy. Unlike grief these feelings do not come in waves, and you may not understand why you feel this way. This can last for weeks, months, or even years if left untreated. Treatment for depression usually involves a combination of lifestyle changes, talking therapies and medicines. Many things can trigger depression such as stressful events, family

history, certain personality types. and even giving birth.
Grief is also a major contributor.

Anxiety

In normal circumstances mild anxiety can be helpful in keeping us safe and help us in avoiding dangerous situations, keeping us alert, and giving us the motivation to deal with problems. Some people have a very identifiable cause for their anxiety for example a traumatic incident or significant loss. We all face challenges as we move through life and in today's society, life is fast, stressful and there is plenty to get anxious and fearful about. A simple effect like caffeine in coffee can often be enough to cause mild anxiety but experiencing a deep loss can potentially create overwhelming feelings of anxiety.

Do you feel constantly anxious?

Do you worry all the time?

Do you always imagine the worst case in every scenario?

Do you overthink about the smallest things?

Do you reject invites to go out?

Do you feel scared constantly of saying something stupid or wrong?

Do you compare yourself to others?

Do you get nervous when you think about the future?

Do you blame yourself when others do not reply to messages?

Do you catastrophise everything?

Do you have trouble falling asleep even when you are sleep deprived?

Do you feel physically and mentally unwell most of the time?

Physical symptoms of anxiety include.

Irregular heartbeats (palpitations)
Sweating
Muscle tension and pains
Breathing heavily
Dizziness
Faintness
Indigestion
Diarrhoea
Tingling in the hands and feet
Tight band across the chest area
Feeling sick
Tension headaches
Hot flushes
Dry mouth
Shaking
Choking sensations

Please seek the advice from your doctor if you are worried about any physical or mental symptoms you may have. You may just need reassurance that you are okay.

Anxiety can alter your perceptions and you may feel you are losing control or going mad. You may think that you are having a heart attack – or you are going to be sick – faint or have a serious illness. You may think you are dying. You may be convinced people are looking at you and observing your anxiety. Your reality may be speeding up or slowing down and it may seem like you are detached from your environment and the people in it. This will leave you feeling on edge and alert to everything around you. You may want to run away thinking you can escape the anxiety.

The most common behavioural symptom of anxiety is avoidance. Although avoiding an anxiety provoking situation produces immediate relief from the anxiety, it is only a short-term solution. This means that whilst it may seem like avoiding is the best thing to do at the time, the anxiety often returns the next time that you face the situation and avoiding it will only psychologically reinforce the message that there is danger. The problem with avoidance is that you never get to find out whether your fear about the situation is real and what would happen if it is actually true. Take back control with the following exercise.

If you feel stuck, please talk to your doctor or therapist but in the meantime, here are some useful hacks to help you move forward.

A grounding exercise to stop an anxiety attack.

1. Look around you.
2. Find five things you can see.
3. Four things you can touch.
4. Three things you can hear.
5. Two things you can smell
6. One thing you can taste.

Tapping into the feel-good hormones.

Dopamine
Eating delicious food, achieving a goal, getting enough sleep, and having a bath are just some of the everyday

activities that you can do to experience a surge of dopamine in the brain. Dopamine is a type of neurotransmitter, and it plays a role in how we feel pleasure. It is commonly known as the happy hormone. Your body makes it, and your nervous system uses it to send messages between nerve cells.

Endorphins

Endorphins are produced naturally by the nervous system to cope with pain or stress. They are often called the "feel-good" chemicals. You can help relieve pain and reduce stress by eating chocolates, drinking wine (in moderation), listening to music, meditating, or having sex! Also, by moving your body and increasing your heart rate with cardiovascular exercise, you can stimulate the production of endorphins in your bloodstream.

Oxytocin

Oxytocin is a hormone and a neurotransmitter that is involved in childbirth and breast-feeding. It is sometimes referred to as the love hormone because levels of oxytocin increase during hugging and orgasm. It is typically linked to warm, fuzzy feelings and shown in some research to lower stress and anxiety. Petting animals is enough to release oxytocin.

Serotonin

You can boost your serotonin levels by having a massage, spending time in nature, getting enough sunshine, practising mindfulness, exercising, and remembering happy events. Serotonin is the key hormone that stabilises mood, feelings of well-being, and happiness. This hormone impacts your entire body. Serotonin also helps with sleeping, eating, and digestion.

Did you know that grief, depression and anxiety can deplete these wonderful hormones?

Depression and anxiety can be part of grief and before we know it, our mindset has been formed and it can seem like an impossible undertaking to be any other way. It is easy to get stuck. Do you feel stuck? Acknowledging that you are stuck is the first step in loosening the problem. Allow it to loosen. Give yourself permission to be a different way. Reach out today for help.

Do you feel ready to loosen your grief?

To create a new way of thinking you need to shift your focus and you can do this by using your imagination and affirmations are a gentle place to start. Also, you can choose to interrupt any dark, sad, or anxious thoughts and patterns as they arise and think about the affirmation you have chosen for the day. Maybe say "no" or "cancel" when an old thought or impulse comes in. Then turn towards the chosen affirmation to keep you moving in the right direction. Build that positive pathway.

Practicing self-compassion and gratitude are powerful ways to kick start these new pathways in your brain. With time, it has been proved, we can literally rewire the neural pathways that control our emotions, thoughts, and reactions

If you are anxious you are living in the future.
If you are depressed, you are living in the past.
If you are at peace you are living in the present.

COMPLEMENTARY THERAPIES
FOR GRIEVERS

Self-care and taking time out for yourself is so important at any time but even more so when you are going through a bereavement. Maybe you do not feel it is appropriate to book a relaxing massage or spa treatment when your world is falling down around you but give yourself a break. You are not being disrespectful to your loved one or the grieving process; you are being disrespectful to yourself by denying yourself time out. The potential benefits will help you to get through the day and they may also have long lasting effects on your mental and physical health and well-being.

So many pressures in life today can make you feel stressed, but the added emotional turmoil of grief can disrupt nearly every system in your body and long-term exposure can lead to serious health issues. It can suppress your immune system, raise your blood pressure, increase the risk of heart attack and stroke, contribute to infertility, and speed up the ageing process. Long-term stress has the potential to rewire your brain, leaving you more vulnerable to depression and anxiety.

Complementary therapies promote relaxation which is perhaps the most important key to your health and well-being. When you are completely relaxed your own natural

healing mechanism is more active. Give yourself
permission to feel relaxed and do something nice for you.

Potential Benefits of Complementary Therapies:
• Reduces stress levels.
• Brings profound relaxation.
• Lowers blood pressure.
• Balances emotions.
• Strengthens the immune system.
• Helps decrease or remove physical pain.
• Calms the anxious and chattering mind.
• Helps to cleanse the body of toxins.
• Strengthens the body's ability to heal itself.

Reiki
Reiki is a Japanese word meaning Universal life
energy. This energy flows in and around all living things.
There are many variations of Reiki but in essence, it is a
healing process that works at bringing you into balance
which reinforces your body's natural ability to heal itself.

The treatment consists of the client lying down fully
clothed on the treatment couch, only removing shoes.
The practitioner then places their hands non-invasively
on the client in a sequence of positions that cover the
body. Reiki energy is then drawn by the client using the
practitioner as a channel.

Clients often experience sensations of warmth,
tingling or chills. Other sensations include feelings of
deep inner peace and harmony, to waves of energy
pulsating throughout the body. Clients often go into such
a relaxed state that they experience waves of colour and
images. At times emotions may be released, but this is

always a very positive experience. Occasionally clients do not experience any sensations during a treatment, but they always feel deeply relaxed afterwards and this in itself aids the body's own natural healing mechanism. Each person will have an individual experience as no two Reiki treatments are the same.

Reflexology

Reflexology is a therapeutic foot massage that aids relaxation and rebalances the body. It revolves around the understanding that there are reflex points on the feet that relate to the structure and function of various parts of the body. Applying pressure to these reflexes using gentle massage may influence the state of the body in many ways. This treatment generally restores the body to a better state so improving physical well-being.

Indian Head Massage

This treatment massages the head, face, neck, shoulders, arms, and hands. The treatment relieves pain and stiffness in the muscles of the face, neck, scalp, shoulders, arms, and upper back. The therapeutic effects also release endorphins (the feel-good chemicals) and this helps to create a feeling of peace and tranquility.

Aromatherapy

Aromatherapy works with the pure properties of plants, using their essential oils in a natural, complementary therapy which can help improve both physical and emotional well-being. It aims to treat the whole person by helping to restore the harmony of mind, body, and spirit. Aromatherapy massage is one of the oldest, simplest forms of therapy and is a system of stroking, pressing, and kneading different areas of the body to relieve pain, relax, stimulate, and tone the muscles. Recommended essential oils for grief include, frankincense, lavender, rose oil, and many of the citrus oils.

Frankincense is a very spiritual essential oil which may help combat depression. It is a comforting oil which calms your mind allowing better clarity in thought. This helps in decision-making difficulties that many people experience during the grieving process. It is also very good at cleansing heavy energies which is why it has been used in religious and spiritual ceremonies for centuries.

Lavender essential oil is one of the most popular and versatile essential oils used in aromatherapy. This oil has a soft floral scent and induces relaxation. It is also used as an excellent antidepressant and mood enhancer.

Rose essential oil encourages self-love and compassion. It is known to strengthen and balance the heart and the heart chakra. This essential oil inspires positive feelings and promotes spiritual growth. It works at soothing grief, healing feelings of despair, and releasing any feelings of trauma or anger. Use it sparingly, as you may get overwhelmed.

Citrus oils such as bergamot, orange, mandarin, and lemon essential oils all have uplifting properties. The bright and cheerful scent encourages you to let go of any heavy energies.
(Always add the essential oils to a base cream or oil. Never use them neat on your skin).

Crystal Therapy

Crystal healing is an energy-based therapy that taps into the energetic power of crystals and how they affect the mind and body. A crystal therapist will place healing crystals on sites of pain or chakras to help unblock, focus, and direct energy. Crystal healing is based on the belief that we are all made up of different energies and that when this becomes stagnant, unbalanced, or blocked, it can cause an imbalance and lead onto physical or mental illness. The premise is that crystals help unblock, balance and direct energy where it is most needed, gently supporting the body to heal in a therapeutic way. Clients remain fully clothed during a session while the therapist places different types of crystals on or around the body. This is a very gentle, comforting therapy. Crystals commonly used for grief include rose quartz, clear quartz, amethyst, and aventurine.

Rose quartz crystal is the stone of unconditional love and infinite peace, and it is the most important stone for the heart and the heart chakra. Its pink colour is symbolic of warmth, love, and gentleness. This crystal calmly draws off heavy energy and replaces it with loving vibes. It opens the heart chakra to all forms of love including self-love, romantic love, family love, and platonic love.

Clear quartz is the most versatile healing crystal known as the master healer. This crystal absorbs stress, releases and regulates energy. It cleanses and enhances the subtle bodies (energy fields) and acts as a deep soul cleanser, connecting the physical dimension with the mind. Clear quartz works on many levels, so is a good all-rounder. This crystal is the most common because of its versatility.

Amethyst quartz crystal is an extremely powerful and protective crystal with a high spiritual vibration. It is a very gentle healing crystal and excellent to use for people with sensitive energy fields. Amethyst crystal is a natural tranquiliser and helps calm the mind. Place an amethyst crystal under your pillow for a good night's sleep. It will also help you to remember your dreams.

Aventurine crystal is known as the heart healer. It is a powerful crystal for calming and healing heavy emotions and it works well with rose quartz bringing balance to the heart centre.

You can incorporate these crystals into your everyday life by keeping them in your pocket, purse, or under your pillow. Alternatively pop them into your water filter or add them to your bath water for general healing.

Sound Bath / Gong Bath

Having a long soak in a warm bubble bath is always relaxing but you can also immerse yourself into the healing vibration of sound.

Typically, a sound bath will involve you lying on a yoga mat fully clothed with a pillow and blanket for comfort. You will be taken on a guided meditation to help you relax, then various sound vibrations and frequencies are created using quartz crystal bowls, Tibetan singing bowls, gongs, and other sound healing instruments. The different sound waves resonate throughout your body, soothing and harmonising your various organs and possibly every cell in your body, bringing you back into balance. These vibrations lead you deeper into a state of contemplation or relaxation, shutting off your body's fight or flight reflex. The frequencies created during a sound bath can potentially trigger a phenomenon called sound healing.

At the end of a session, your provider will guide you back to a feeling of awareness before concluding the sound bath and wishing you well on your journey.

(I am only highlighting the various treatments I offer but there are many other therapies and treatments available to support your physical and mental well-being.)

Falling down is part of life but getting back up is a choice.

THE MOUNTAIN MEDITATION FOR THE BEREAVED

Adapted from Jon Kabat- Zinn's version.

This is normally done in the sitting position.

Some people like to record this on their phone so they can listen and follow the guided narration.

Find a comfortable position and place your hands on your lap.

And when you are ready, lower your gaze or allow your eyes to close.

Notice any sounds outside the room.

Notice any sounds within the room.

Become aware of the space around you.

Allow your body to be still, sitting with a sense of dignity, a sense of resolve, sitting upright with a straight back.

Become aware of your breath as it enters and leaves your body.

Breathing through your nose notice the physical sensations with each breath - letting the breath be just as it is - without trying to change it in any way - allowing it to flow easily and naturally - with its own rhythm and pace.

As you sit here - imagine in your mind's eye the most magnificent, beautiful mountain.

Let it gradually come into focus - if it doesn't come as a visual image, allow the sense of this mountain with its overall shape to find you.

The mountain has lofty peaks high in the sky.

The large base is rooted in the bedrock of the earth's crust.

It may have steep or gently sloping sides.

Notice how massive the mountain is - how solid - how unmoving - how beautiful - whether from afar - or up close.

Perhaps your mountain has snow blanketing the top - and trees reaching down to the base - or rugged granite sides.

There may be streams and waterfalls cascading down the slopes.

There may be one peak or several peaks - with meadows and high lakes.

Observe the mountain - noting its qualities.

When you feel ready - see if you can bring the mountain into your own body - so that your body and the mountain in your mind's eye become one - so that as you sit here - you share in the massiveness and the stillness and majesty of the mountain - you become the mountain.

Grounded in the sitting posture - your head becomes the lofty peak - supported by the rest of the body and affording a panoramic view.

Your shoulders and arms are the sides of the mountain.

Your thighs and legs the solid base - rooted to your cushion or your chair.

With each breath - as you continue sitting - become one with the mountain.

The mountain breathing as you breath - unwavering in your inner stillness.

You are the mountain.

The mountain is you.

As you sit here - becoming aware that the sun travels across the sky - the light and shadows and colours are changing moment by moment in the mountain's stillness - and the surface teems with life and activity – streams - melting snow – waterfalls - plants and wildlife.

As the mountain sits - seeing and feeling how night follows day - and day follows night.

The bright warming sun - followed by the cool night sky studded with stars - and the gradual dawning of a new day.

Through it all - the mountain just sits - experiencing change in each moment - constantly

changing - yet always just being itself.

The mountain remains still as the seasons flow into one another - and as the weather changes moment by moment - day by day - the mountain remains still.

In summer, there is no snow on the mountain except perhaps for the peaks or in crags shielded from direct sunlight.

In the autumn, the mountain may wear a coat of brilliant fire colours.

In winter, a blanket of snow and ice.

In any season, it may find itself at times enshrouded in clouds or fog or pelted by freezing rain.

People may come to see the mountain and comment on how beautiful it is - or how it's not a good day to see the mountain - or that it's too cloudy or wet or foggy or dark.

None of this matters to the mountain – as it remains at all times neutral.

Clouds may come and clouds may go - tourists may like it or not like it.

The mountain's magnificence and beauty are not changed one bit by whether people see it or not - seen or unseen - in sun or clouds, boiling or freezing, day or night.

It just sits, being itself.

At times visited by violent storms, buffeted by snow and rain and winds of unthinkable magnitude.

Through it all, the mountain sits.

Spring comes, tree's leaf out, flowers bloom in the high meadows and slopes, birds sing in the trees once again. Streams overflow with the waters of melting snow.

Through it all - the mountain continues to sit - unmoved by the weather - by what happens on its surface - by the world of appearances - remaining its essential self - through the seasons - the changing weather - the activity ebbing and flowing on its surface.

In the same way - as we sit in meditation - we can learn to experience the mountain - we can embody the same central unwavering stillness - feeling grounded - in the face of everything that changes in our own lives.

In our lives and in our meditation practice - we experience the constant changing nature of our mind and body and of the outer world - we have our own periods of light and darkness - activity and inactivity - our moments of colour and our moments of gloom.

It's true that we experience storms of varying intensity and violence in our outer world - and in our own minds and bodies - buffeted by high winds - by cold and rain - we endure periods of darkness and pain - as well as moments of joy - even our appearance changes constantly - experiencing a weather of its own.

By becoming the mountain in our meditation practice - we can link up with its strength and stability and adopt them for our own. We can use the mountain's energies to support our energy to encounter each moment with mindfulness and calmness and clarity.

It may help us to see that our thoughts and feelings - our preoccupations - our emotional storms and crises - all the things that happen to us are very much like the weather on the mountain.

The weather of our own lives is not to be ignored or denied - it is to be encountered - and held in awareness.

And in holding it in this way - we come to know a deeper silence and stillness and wisdom.

Mountains have this to teach us and much more if we can let it in.

So, if you find you resonate in some way with the strength and stability of the mountain in your sitting - it may be helpful to use it from time to time in your meditation practice – to remind you of what it means to sit mindfully with resolve and with wakefulness - in true stillness.

Continue to sit here and feel the qualities of this mountain – absorbing its strength – resilience – feeling grounded – calm – and at peace.

Pause

And now it is time to come back.

Start to wiggle your fingers and toes.

Become aware of the space around you and the room you are in.

When you feel ready, bring this meditation to a close and open your eyes.

Notice how you feel.

This meditation can be downloaded FREE from my website.

GRIEF AFFIRMATIONS

Positive affirmations are short and powerful phrases that you say to yourself when you need a little mental or spiritual boost. Everyone needs a *pick me up* now and then. In time, these phrases can potentially become your thoughts, which can support you in moving forward in a more positive way. They help to create a resilient mindset that in turn helps you cope with your grief and loss. They influence the conscious and unconscious mind and as a result, your behaviour, your thoughts, and your actions prevent you from becoming stuck.

Affirmations help bring up associated mental images into your mind, which inspire, energise, and motivate you. Repeating an affirmation throughout the day may help you move through your sorrow. You do not need to memorise these phrases, but it does help if you write them down on sticky post it notes and place them on your mirrors, fridge door, or other areas to remind yourself to use them. Healing takes time, and with each passing month, the pain of your loss will begin to ease. Use the following affirmations as a helpful tool for dealing with the intense feelings of grief and loss to bring clarity into the present moment.

Affirmations:

I allow the pain in my heart to heal.

The pain in your heart will heal but how you process your experience of grief and loss will determine how quickly this happens. Nobody else can do this for you. There may be a part of you that dies when your loved one passes away but your heart will mend itself. Trust that it will.

Grief has changed me and change is okay.

When you lose a loved one it changes you forever. It is difficult to accept that you may no longer be the same person you were before. People may want to reassure you and say that things will go back to normal in time, and that everything will be fine. The reality is that a new normal is waiting for you. Life will never be the same again and grief will change you. You will become a more updated version of your old self.

I choose to hold on to love.

When the physical body dies and we lose a loved one, the love we have for that person continues but it feels like the love has nowhere to go. Love cannot cease to exist, and the bond cannot be broken. Love is infinite. In time, you will understand that your feelings of love are stronger, and this can help you overcome your darkest days. The pain of your grief will ebb and flow, but it is safe to hold on to love and let go of grief.

Today I am grateful for the memories.

When someone you love has died, focus your energy on remembering all the love and joy they brought into your life. The memories you have are the gifts they left behind for you to keep. You will treasure these gifts forever. Feel gratitude for these memories. These memories will save you.

I am transforming.

There are various phases of grief that you will experience, and everyone has their unique way of going through the process. Grief will change you. Allow yourself to be transformed. You will still be the same person but with an upgrade. When you choose to see it as a transformation it may help you feel you have more control.

Grief reminds me that I loved a special person.

Deep loss is the price for deep love. Feel gratitude for the experience of deep love. Some people go through their whole lives and never experience this. Would you have chosen a life without it? Accept the pain of missing them but feel appreciation for the love they brought into your life.

I release the tension in my body, and I choose to feel relaxed.

Where are you holding tension in your body? Is it in your shoulders, your face, or somewhere else? Maybe it feels like it is everywhere. Just notice it and give yourself permission to relax and let it go. You have the control to do this. Take in a long slow deep breath and then as you breathe out slowly, relax your body, from the top of your head to the tips of your fingers and toes. Repeat and relax!

I give myself permission to feel happy today.

It may be the smell of a cup of coffee or seeing a beautiful flower. It may be a strangers smile or the feel of the sun on your skin or the sound of nature. Allow yourself to feel happy even if it is for a fleeting moment. You can build on this the more you practise this affirmation. You do not have to wait for things to get easier because life will always be complicated.

I choose to feel the presence of my loved one.

Close your eyes and remember their face, their voice, their laugh, their smell, their energy. Imagine they are standing next to you now giving you a virtual hug. Feel the essence of them surrounding you. Feel the love you have for each other and really connect with their presence.

I choose to feel at peace today.

Feeling at peace is feeling calm, feeling grounded, acknowledging your pain and being able to sit with it in a peaceful, loving way. You are in control of how you feel from one moment to the next. When you find moments of peace, this sends our loved ones peace too. You may not want to feel at peace today and that's fine – you can choose another affirmation.

I choose to find peace with uncertainty.

Feeling uncertain has a different energy to accepting uncertainty. Nobody knows what the future holds but accepting uncertainty is about meeting life where it is and moving forward from there. Sometimes the best thing you can do is not think, not wonder, nor imagine, or obsess. Just breathe and trust that everything will work out for the best. Maybe not how you planned it, but just how it's meant to be. It is time to make peace with uncertainty.

I choose to find peace with the present moment.
The past has gone, and the future is yet to come but the present moment, as you read these words, is here and now. Choose to find peace in this present moment and notice how it feels. Breathe slowly and deeply and notice the sounds around you. Become aware of the space around you. Just enjoy a moment of peace, now. Peace is waiting for you.

I trust that all is well.
Life will be what it will be and trying to control or resist it will cause more emotional distress. When you learn to trust that all is well, you will feel much more relaxed. You already trust that your lungs will breathe, and your heart will pump. The sun will set tonight and rise again tomorrow. The tide will come in and the tide will go out. Transfer that same trust to other areas of your life and have faith that all is well.

I choose to find peace in the mystery.
While you learn that some things in life will never make sense, you have the capacity to find peace in the mystery. Peace is about retraining your mind to process life as it is and not as you think it should be. The mystery is okay. It is safe to not understand everything. Life is what it is, and the mystery can be wonderful.

I choose to feel hopeful today.
Hope is the belief that the future may be better. Not necessarily tomorrow, or next week, or next month but

sometime in the future. If we believe the future may be better, we can cope with today. Hope is a feeling of expectation and desire which increases the sense of meaning in life. It is safe to feel hope. Give yourself permission to feel hopeful today.

I allow the waves of grief to wash over me today.
Grief comes in waves. Over time as you process your grief and loss you will notice the space in between each wave. At first the space may seem like a pause in time, and it may feel dull, empty, painful, etc. The space is important. The lull between each wave gives you a window of opportunity to breathe. To be. Sit with this space. Feel the calm. Breathe. Peace is waiting for you between the waves.

HAPPY JOURNAL

When my son first passed away, I could not look through the family photograph albums without falling apart. In the early days everything was a trigger. During this time a close friend of mine made me a beautiful scrapbook which was presented in a decorated box. It was a blank scrapbook designed for me to use as a journal or photograph album. Each page was hand made with card and beautifully decorated. Some pages included pockets for keeping small items. I decided to call it my happy journal.

"I'm grieving for God's sake, why would I have a happy journal?"

I collect inspirational poems, positive affirmations, phrases, pictures, and anything else that makes me feel good. I leave it on my coffee table and from time to time, I flick through the pages, and it makes me smile. By connecting with the positive content in my happy journal it lifts my spirit, and it helps to brighten my day. I am now on my second happy journal as my first one is full.

I recommend everyone has their own individual happy journal. Filling your happy journal is as important as completing your journal. While you are collecting and looking for inspirational information to add, this helps to change your mood. It is a healthy resource to keep you moving in the right direction.

At the start of each day there is a moment I realise something is missing.

Sometimes it's okay and sometimes it isn't.

It feels like not being home, yet I yearn to find home one more time.

That is grief and loss!

A LETTER TO MY GRIEF

Dear Grief,

I knew you were coming. You've visited me before but even though I knew you were coming this time; I wasn't prepared for you to do your worse. You can be brutal can't you? Where do you come from? Were you lurking just around the corner, with the grim reaper, waiting for a tragedy to strike? Do you feed off my sadness? Do you enjoy and embrace your role? When you've done your job, will you leave me?

We have been to the darkest depths of my soul together and you have seen me at my worst. I was forced to go on this journey, and you have been like super glue every step of the way. I'm through the worst of it now and I want you to know that. We have come a long way together and although you feel like the enemy, we have become old friends. Sometimes I forget you are there and in those brief moments, I panic. How could I forget you? We have developed a close partnership even though I hated you in the beginning. You made me furious, and you tried to break me. Remember those days? There was so much pain in my life and I wanted to die to escape you, but I'm still here and I'm starting to like you now.

I am broken but also mended like a mosaic. I have pieced myself back together and I feel whole again but the cement holding me together is still wet. It is drying but at my speed because I need some control. You controlled the situation for far too long and it's my turn now, but don't leave me. Please don't feel your job is done and abandon me. I am happy with this current version of me, and I will continue to update myself as I move forward in my life, but I want to keep holding your hand. I don't want to lose you yet.

Is it possible to grieve the loss of grief? Who grieves for you? I will keep you close, somewhere safe inside and I will love you. There is a home here for as long as you want. I will nurture you and keep you safe. Thank you for being here. You are proof I loved and lost a special person. Is it wrong to start feeling grateful for you? Is that too weird? You haven't replaced my son and never will but there will always be a place inside for you. You are part of me now and I kinda like that. We can live together and share this body and experience this thing called life.

Can we have a ceasefire please and make peace with each other? I'd like that.

Dearest grief, you have bought so much into my life, please forgive me, I am sorry, thank you, I love you.

Louise Bates

"If light is in your heart, you will find your way home." Rumi

EMOTIONAL FREEDOM TECHNIQUES (EFT) AND MATRIX REIMPRINTING

Throughout my first book 'Letters to Matthew – Life After Loss' I wrote about various techniques that I use in my private complementary therapy practice. These include a tapping technique, known as the Emotional Freedom Techniques (EFT) and Matrix Reimprinting.

EFT is a constantly evolving technique of which there are many variations, but it is commonly known as Tapping Therapy.

Essentially these techniques address the entire mind – body system and explore how you process your thoughts, emotions, beliefs, and past experiences along with how your body responds.

EFT combines a simple but amazingly effective set of techniques which can release trapped emotions and potentially clear years of emotional baggage. It became an invaluable tool which helped to heal my broken heart after my son Matthew died. I had to be ready to work with this because in the early days when I felt broken by the rawness of grief, I did not want to do anything. I was not looking to be mended. I needed to experience my emotions and feel everything that grief had to throw at me. It is important to acknowledge that EFT is a very transformative technique and grief cannot be rushed.

Eventually, when I felt ready, I decided to work on myself using EFT and I became my own grief therapist. I also incorporated Matrix Reimprinting.

Matrix Reimprinting is the evolution of EFT.

The theory behind Matrix Reimprinting is that our unconscious minds are all connected through what we call the Matrix or the Field: an understanding common to many philosophies and cultures. The Matrix is a quantum dimension which holds all our individual selves, past, present, and future. We call these selves, ECHOs (Energetic Consciousness Holograms). Once in the Matrix, we can communicate with our ECHOs and also other people, including our loved ones who have passed over.

Working with Matrix Reimprinting enabled me to re-visit my son's cancer journey and interact with my ECHOs. I could not change the past or what happened, but I could change how I perceived any past events. I was then able to resolve the trauma and change my perception of my negative memories.

By connecting and communicating with your ECHOs, you can understand the decisions you made at the time and then create more resourceful interpretations. This changes how you hold it inside. Together with your ECHO you can generate new pictures and new feelings which create new positive emotions. You can also work with your future ECHOs too.

I was holding onto some very painful memories I had of Matthew regarding his two years of illness, his treatments, experiences, and his death. These were memories I could not even talk about without becoming deeply distraught. Matrix Reimprinting allowed me to gently re-visit these dark memories and, in doing that, I connected with my son.

Matthew popped into the Matrix time after time, reassuring me he is not suffering now. Each time, I could see his smiling face reminding me that he is not in that memory. Each time we connected, he would say, *"Come on Mum, you know this stuff. Why are you hanging onto it? Let it go. I'm not there now."* To see him looking so peaceful and happy and to hear his voice gave me enormous comfort.

I healed the most painful memories easily and in such a short amount of time, which to some people, would seem impossible. And by knocking out the negative emotional intensity of the big ones, lots of other painful memories just collapsed too. When I think of those particular memories now, I see Matthew's smiling face, I hear his voice reassuring me, and I know he is transformed, and so am I.

Imagine you could travel back in time and have a conversation with your younger self. What would you say? The Matrix Reimprinting process allows you to do this. Imagine you could travel into your future too. The Matrix or Field is a place of unlimited potential, as I discovered through my own experiences.

Some people may say I imagined my experiences or that it is just fluffy whoo-hoo nonsense, but it was real for me, and it made a massive difference in how I experienced my grief journey and in the end that is all that matters. Whatever works for you is the important thing, and everyone has a choice in which path to take.

Matrix Reimprinting and other types of tapping therapy are not the cure for grief, because there is no cure, but these techniques helped me to heal my heart and I learned how to carry, experience and care for my grief. I became more emotionally resilient, grounded, and balanced which created a space for me to feel the connection to Matthew.

Through EFT and Matrix Reimprinting I discovered different perceptions and insights which cultivated a new awareness of just how powerful I AM.

For more information about these incredible techniques check out these links:

www.heathcoteholistics.co.uk/eft
www.energyeft.com
www.matrixreimprinting.com
www.emofree.com

Hope is hope!
If we believe that tomorrow will be better, we can cope with today.

CLIENT CASE STUDIES

(Names and situations have been changed to protect the identity of each client)

I work as an Emotional Freedom Techniques (EFT) and Matrix Reimprinting Practitioner. EFT is commonly known as tapping therapy, and it is my passion. I have helped countless clients over the years with various issues but supporting people through a bereavement must be the most rewarding.

Anne's Loss

Anne had been married to her husband for fifty-five years. Since his death she had been to counselling and psychotherapy to help deal with her grief, but she was still struggling six years later.

Her husband had become very ill two years before his death, and she was still angry about the care he had received. She felt his care had not been good enough and that he had been very badly let down by the health care service. She had spent the last six years since his death focusing on her husband's lack of care, his illness, and all he went through. She shared various scenarios with me that still haunted her. They were scenarios that went through her mind every day. Little did she know that while she played these events over and over in her mind constantly day after day, month after month, she was giving them more and more power. She was making them stronger with each replay and in doing this she got angrier and angrier. Her anger was keeping her stuck in grief.

After a while, I asked her what her husband was like? Her face instantly softened, and she described the kindest, most gentle, loving soul to me. He was generous, funny, and he was her soul mate. She told me about their wonderful marriage, their three beautiful children and two grandchildren, and about all the amazing places they had travelled to throughout the world. She had so many beautiful memories. While she talked about this her whole-body language changed. She relaxed, she smiled, she laughed, and her energy felt wonderful.

We chatted for a while about what a lovely life she had had with her husband.

After a while, I pointed out to her that while she spoke about her husband and her marriage and all the wonderful things they had done together, how she had changed, how she relaxed, smiled, laughed, and softened. I reminded her that they had had fifty-five wonderful years together but for the last six years she had only focused her attention on the last two years of his life. She had focused on her husband's illness, the lack of care, and all the scenarios that made her angry.

I asked her if she was ready to release her anger, and she said that she was, so we did some tapping therapy together to help her release the anger.

We condition ourselves sometimes to focus on the negative scenarios for various reasons, but these unhealthy thoughts and emotions do not fix anything. Negative thoughts create more negative emotions which feed anxiety and depression etc. During Anne's bereavement she had been hanging on to so much anger and negative emotion about her husband's care that she stopped focusing on the fifty-five years of happiness that they had spent together.

Anne cannot change the fact that she felt her husband's care was not good enough. What she can do is write to the appropriate people and express her concerns in the hope that changes are made, and other people do not suffer as she believes her husband did.

After just one session, Anne felt lighter, happier, more relaxed, and positive about her future. I gave her some work to do at home which involved practising her good memories and after five sessions with me she felt in a good enough place to not need any more support.

Losing her husband will always be sad and there is no cure for this, but she gave herself permission to let go of the anger which had kept her stuck in her grief. She reprogrammed her mind to focus on the fifty-five wonderful, happy years her and her hubby had shared together and she was able to move on in a much more positive way.

When grief is new and raw it is natural to focus on the negative events around the death of your loved one. It is your mind's way of trying to make sense of an awful situation. Your life has been broken into tiny pieces and you are trying to put it all back together, but it can never go back together.

If you are still replaying negative thoughts years later with the same intensity you may be stuck in your grief. I can still get angry about the way my son Matthew was treated during his illness. We saw the best and the worst of the National Health Service and some instances still haunt me five years on as I write this book. I am still a work in progress, but I am learning to focus my attention on the joy Matthew brought into our lives. We had many years of happy times, and I am grateful for the memories. I am still working on myself and learning to let go and grief is not a straight line. No-one can change what happened, but we can change how we feel about it.

Patricia's Loss

Patricia came to me because she was experiencing overwhelming anxiety and panic attacks.

After an initial consultation we chatted about her life in general when suddenly she opened up to me and explained that her eldest child had been murdered many years ago. The session went in a very different direction after this.

She had never had therapy before, and she was very surprised to be talking about her son's murder. She had not planned on opening up about this but as a therapist I am prepared for these moments as they happen from time to time. A client can come in for one reason, but then lots of other reasons come to the surface.

She went on to explain that after her son was murdered over sixty years ago, she stopped talking about him. She said everyone did. It was awkward and messy and easier to avoid those conversations. Obviously, police were involved as well as the court hearing and everything else that happens with a murder investigation. Her innocent son had been in the wrong place at the wrong time, and he was taken too soon.

When a loved one is murdered, you not only mourn your loss, but you are also traumatized by it. Patricia had never had any professional support before and here she was talking to me and sharing her experience and I felt very honoured. It was a sacred special experience.

"What was your son like," I asked. Patricia described a quiet, sensitive, loving boy and as she carried on, she relaxed even more. It was a safe moment for her to share how proud she was of having such a wonderful son. She had probably not had a chance to do this in years. She told me funny stories about him, what he used to get up to and what he liked to eat.

We did some tapping therapy together. While she talked about her son, I felt the energy in the room change. It was filled with a loving presence as if her son was with us in that moment. Patricia felt it too. It was an emotional moment but we both felt the connection.

After one session Patricia said she felt like a different person. She had felt close to her son for the first time since he died, and the experience had lifted her spirit. We talked about how important it is to keep our loved one's memory alive and I encouraged Patricia to talk to her other grown-up children about their brother. Conversations do not have to focus on the pain and sadness of the events that led to his death. They can share the good memories and remember the funny, happy times. They can talk about the triumphs of life despite their loss. It does not have to feel uncomfortable and clumsy. They are grieving too and may need to talk. She can honour her son by connecting to the love inside she still holds for him. That bond can never be broken. I believe that when you fully immerse yourself into this energy you will send them peace beyond belief.

Patricia had five sessions with me and during these sessions she released a lot of negative emotion. The first session was the most intense but also the most amazing. Eventually her anxiety decreased, and the panic attacks disappeared.

A few years later I bumped into Patricia in the supermarket, and she gave me the biggest hug. She had heard that I had lost my son Matthew and she passed on her condolences. She told me how much her sessions with me had helped her and I told her how much they had helped me too. Patricia was proof to me that if she could learn to move on through her life after such an awful loss, it was possible for me to do the same. Patricia you are an inspiration!

(Do you know someone who has lost a very important person in their life? Are you afraid to mention their name in case you make them feel sad? You cannot make them feel sad because they are already sad. When you mention their name, you are remembering that they lived and that is a comfort and a great gift.)

Sonia's Loss

Sonia came to me after the birth of her first child. She had experienced a perfect pregnancy and birth and she loved her new role of being a mother.

Sonia explained that not long after the birth she started thinking about an abortion she had had many years earlier. Her partner at the time was not happy about her being pregnant and she felt unsupported. She made the decision that the timing was not right, and she had an abortion. She hadn't thought twice about it since but now as a new mother, lots of negative thoughts were coming up for her. *Had she done the right thing? How old would that baby be now?* Thoughts started to haunt her, and it was taking away the pleasure of being a new mum.

We talked about what was going on for her at the time when she decided to make that decision and logically, she knew she had done the right thing. I explained that maybe she was now experiencing a type of delayed loss, triggered by the birth of her new baby. Maybe pregnancy hormones were also affecting her thought processes too. We didn't need to understand the reasons why she felt this way for Sonia to make peace with her actions. I asked her if she was ready to let this issue go, and she said that she was, so we did some tapping therapy together. We talked about her beliefs around birth and death, and we discussed various philosophies. While we were working together through her issue, Sonia suddenly became very emotional.

She said that while we were working together, she got a realisation, a mental download, an aha moment, that the soul of her first baby could not be born because the pregnancy was terminated but the soul waited for her to get pregnant again. The thought that her baby's soul waited for her next pregnancy completely changed how she felt about her abortion. She said it was like a spiritual message. This experience completely uplifted Sonia and she stopped feeling bad about having an abortion many years previously.

(Whether a client believes in souls or not is not for me to judge. In this case it was a healthy and happy outcome for Sonia, and I had done my job.)

After an abortion, it is normal to feel relief, sadness, grief, or guilt. These feelings can vary from woman to woman. Natural hormonal changes that occur in your body during pregnancy are affected by an abortion. These hormonal changes can make you feel more emotional than usual. It is okay to feel what you feel. It is safe to feel these emotions, but it is not healthy to push them down or put a lid on them. Process them and give yourself permission to let them go.

John's Loss

John came to me because he was struggling with the loss of his pet dog. His dog had been his constant companion for nearly 16 years, and he was heartbroken to lose him. It had been six months since the loss, and he was struggling to come to terms with it.

In terms of grief, six months is nothing. When a pet has been part of your daily life for so long, you are not going to recover in six months.

We did some tapping therapy on how he felt and that managed to lighten and loosen the load. He gave himself permission to grieve as long as he wanted to, putting no pressure on himself about when he should be over it. We chatted about ways he could honour his dog and he told me about his plans to scatter his dog's ashes in his favourite place. I gave him space to talk about his dog and how he felt, which for a lot of pet owners is what they need. Society does tend to trivialise pet loss and people feel they cannot talk about it.

John only needed one session. He needed someone to hear him and validate his feelings. He accepted that grief was the price for being in love with another sentient being. It was normal to feel whatever he was feeling, and it was healthy to acknowledge and process what was going on for him.

Many pet owners often feel disenfranchised grief by the loss of their pet, as they grieve deeply but also feel they cannot take time off work, or do not know who to talk to about the way they feel. Our pets are part of our family but not everyone understands that, especially people who do not own pets. Often those experiencing disenfranchised grief may feel isolated, stigmatised, and ashamed. It is important to find someone that understands your loss and how you feel.

John left the session feeling lighter and more at peace with his grief. He still had a way to go but he was moving in the right direction.

Gillian's Loss

Gillian had lost her older sister when she was ten years old. Her sister had been born with serious health issues and had spent much of her childhood in and out of hospital. Gillian was now married and in her forties with children of her own. She explained that as she got older, the more she thought about her loss, and it was starting to negatively impact her daily life.

We chatted about memories of her sister how she felt about her loss now. There were lots of negative emotions in the mix. Guilt because she felt she never received the attention she deserved as a child. Anger because her sisters death changed the dynamics of her family. Sadness because her sister died, and she also witnessed her parents' grief. Fear that she may lose one of her own children. So many negative thoughts and emotions that she had been carrying around with her for the last thirty years and it was beginning to weigh her down. She felt she could not talk to her parents as it would upset them, and her husband couldn't understand why she was still upset about something that happened so many years ago.

I asked Gillian to think about each emotion and tune into each feeling. Where could she feel them in her body. The guilt, the anger, the sadness, and fear. We did tapping therapy on each of these emotions, and it was incredible how quickly she started to release these emotions.

We did some work on connecting with the memory of her sister. The good memories, the family holidays, the birthdays, and Christmases when her sister was still around. She had been a good sister. She remembered helping her mum care for her sister. She remembered reading her stories and cuddling her. By releasing all the negative emotions, her good memories started to rise to the surface and happy flashbacks took their place.

She connected to her younger self through matrix reimprinting, and she could see first-hand how perfect she was. What a perfect sister and daughter she had been, and she started to make peace with her past.

She gave herself permission to release and let go a lot of negative emotions and she changed her unhealthy beliefs and perceptions that had built up over a thirty-year period. By making peace with her grief, she was now able to live a happier more fulfilling life. Through the tapping and matrix work, she is now able to focus her attention on remembering the happy family times. It will always be sad that Gillian lost her sister, and nothing can change that, but I do believe that when we are able to make peace with our loss, it sends peace to our loved ones too. Gillian only needed three sessions.

The death of a sibling not only changes the family forever, but it changes the relationship with the parents and the siblings. Sibling loss is rarely talked about, and children can be easily traumatised. It is upsetting to see your parents cry and many parents try to protect their children by hiding their emotions, but children pick up on everything. When children see their parents upset and going through the pain of grief it turns their safe world upside down, but communication is the key. Usually, the parents are so busy trying to cope with their own pain that it is hard to also deal with how their children are coping. Professional help is so beneficial when children are involved. Fortunately, nowadays there are amazing charities that can help support families through these scenarios.

Jack's Loss

Jack had been adopted by a lovely family when he was only a couple of weeks old, and he had had what he describes as a perfect upbringing. He was an only child and very happy in his family, but he always wondered why he had been adopted. He wanted more detail. He was told that his mum was very young when she had him and that she was unable to care for him. He had a black and white photo of his mum holding him as a baby which he treasured. He had never tried to find his mum because he didn't want to upset his adoptive parents, but he wanted help in what he described as 'unpleasant emotions inside'. He said the 'unpleasant emotions inside' were getting bigger and he wanted to put a lid on it.

As a therapist I would never assist a client on putting a lid on anything other than a saucepan! Buried emotions never go away, they sit there in the body and life events can trigger them reminding you that they are still there bubbling away under the surface.

We all have emotional baggage of some sort. We can push it down, forget about it, or think, I'll sort that out later, but if we don't process it, it will keep reminding us that it is still there. We may go through life collecting more emotional baggage, adding it to all the other stuff pushed down and it can potentially affect our health and well-being. It can cause anxieties, depression, and all sorts of mental health issues.

Jack had gone through his life missing his birth mother. He had always wondered why she had given him up and over the years it had grown into an unhealthy perspective that his mum hadn't wanted him, and he felt abandoned. Deep down he wanted to find his mother and connect with her and ultimately find out why he had been adopted.

He had never shared his thoughts and emotions about his issue to anyone before and he was very anxious talking about it. We did a lot of tapping therapy to release his anxieties and to help him relax into the session.

Once he relaxed, we talked about his 'unpleasant emotions inside'. I needed to know how old he was when he first noticed the unpleasant emotions inside. I needed to know how intense the unpleasant emotions felt inside for him – in that moment. He needed to connect to the unpleasant emotions for a short while in order to release them. Feeling is healing. We did a lot of tapping therapy on this, and it reduced quite significantly. We also did some amazing work using matrix reimprinting where he connected to himself as a baby. It was a very intense emotional session for him but incredibly healing for him too.

There were so many aspects feeding into his issue but after three sessions Jack had made peace with his adoption and with his birth mother. The 'unpleasant emotions inside' had gone and he felt more in control of his feelings. He felt more resilient and able to move forward in his life and confident about one day connecting with his birth mother.

My First Therapy Session

I was reluctant to go to therapy because being a therapist myself surely I should be able to sort myself out? I felt embarrassed and I resisted for a long time. I also felt that I did not want to heal because the pain felt like the last link to Matthew.

Eventually I chose to see a dear friend who is also an EFT practitioner. He encouraged me to do tapping therapy sessions with him and thank goodness I took him up on his kind offer. As a therapist I had been working with EFT myself for years and it felt more comfortable to me than the traditional talking therapies.

I turned up at my first session anxious and scared not knowing where to start. My friend quickly made me feel relaxed and we started to chat. I explained that I had no idea where to begin.

I had watched my son Matthew deteriorate over a period of two years due to his cancer diagnosis and I had never experienced anxiety like it before. He had been back and forth to the doctors for months, but they did not seem to be concerned. I knew he was ill so insisted I went into the doctors with him which he was very embarrassed about. I told the doctor that something was wrong and that was the point they started to take him seriously. After a few tests and scans they found a 13cm tumour on his kidney. Matthew was diagnosed with cancer and our lives changed forever.

We faced the best and the worst of the National Health Service system during these two years. This encouraged me to investigate every alternative and complementary treatment out there in search for the cure. I bought organic fruit and vegetables and juiced and cooked all the foods that are supposed to support the body back to health. I sourced illegal cannabis oil. I devoured any book I could find on healing cancer. I searched websites and looked for other patients that had cured themselves of kidney cancer. I needed to know how they did it because I knew it was possible. Matthew was happy for me to do this, and I wanted him to relax and concentrate on enjoying himself. I became a mum on a mission but the constant hospital appointments, cancelled appointments, medical cock ups, and everyday stress and anxiety that cancer bought into our lives took its toll on all of us.

The constant worry became our natural default setting. We ran on empty month after month from lack of sleep. The panic and fear of what a new scan would reveal or what a new day would bring was overwhelming. Watching your child in pain knowing there is nothing you can do about it is torture. Just when we thought, it could not get any worse, Matthew died.

The grief – What can I say? For those who understand no explanation is needed. For those who do not understand, no explanation is possible.

Here I was in my first therapy session - where the bloody hell do I start?

"How do you feel?" My tapping buddy asked me.

"I feel like there is a big hole in the middle of my torso. It is so big you can see through it." I replied.

"Well let's start there," he said.

We started EFT tapping therapy on this big hole in the middle of my torso. I felt strange at first and a bit spaced out and a bit numb. I was following the tapping procedure not even sure how I felt, but I was just going through the motions. After a few rounds of tapping something incredible happened. I saw Matthew's face smiling back at me. I could telepathically hear his voice in my head saying, *"Come on mum, you know this stuff, let it go, I'm fine now."* It felt so real to me in that moment, and I became emotional. It was happy tears though as this felt like Matthew was giving me permission to let it go. He kept repeating, *"It's okay mum, let it go."*

When we finished the last round, my tapping buddy asked me, *"How is the hole in your torso now?"* I checked in, and to my amazement I could not see or feel that hole in my torso. I was feeling ecstatic after seeing my son's smiling face and hearing his voice in my head and I shared my experience with my tapping buddy. To my astonishment, my tapping buddy had also had the same experience. He had picked up on Matthew's message too!

This was the start of my healing journey. This one session had loosened my grief and in doing this I connected to my son. I went back every two weeks for more tapping, and I had lots of other extraordinary experiences and my journey is still ongoing.

EFT Tapping Therapy is not the cure for grief because there is no cure, but it will help to loosen it. It certainly keeps me moving in the right direction.

Did I make contact with my son Matthew? I believe I did.

EFT is able to reduce or remove the emotional impact of memories and incidents that trigger emotional distress. It is a technique that can clear years of emotional baggage. Emotional baggage is your trapped emotions. The fact that I believe my message from Matthew was real was an added unexpected bonus.

GRIEF AND THERAPY

Therapy is not about fixing you or forcing the healing process. It is about being there for you, supporting you, hearing you, acknowledging your pain and guiding you as you navigate your way forward.

A therapist doesn't just hold you in their mind for the hour or so that you sit in front of them. They research topics related to your case outside of sessions. They spend hours doing notes and treatment plans for you and they hold you in their thoughts between sessions. It may be difficult to talk to your friends and family so talking to a therapist may be easier and therapists do care deeply.

I believe everyone needs therapy. You do not need to wait until a negative life event happens.

Healing and growth are a continual process but sometimes it is easy to get stuck. You may need a gentle nudge to loosen the problem and there is no shame in enlisting professional support. Some issues may take longer to resolve than others but that's not because of their intensity or longevity. Rather it is because of their complexity, for example, the number of aspects involved. Aspects are different parts of the issue that contribute to the emotional intensity. A trained therapist can recognise and assist in dealing with these problems helping you to move forward.

Grief counselling or therapy aims to help people cope with the physical, emotional, social, spiritual, and cognitive responses to their loss. For people who are facing grief alone, therapy sessions validate their feelings and provide a safe space to fully express emotions. Several family members or couples can attend counselling sessions together if they wish to learn how to support each other more effectively.

Grief counselling and therapy provides people with an understanding, supportive, and non-judgmental space to explore their thoughts, feelings, and emotions that come up after the loss of a loved one. People may be more open to fully expressing their emotions with a trained professional who validates their experience.

The human experience of grief cannot be side-tracked; it must be felt.

Working as a therapist I understood the techniques and tools used to help people travel through bereavement but when my son Matthew died, I didn't want to use them on myself. I wanted to sit in my grief and feel every ounce of pain caused by his death. Grief cannot be rushed!

It took me a few months before I enlisted the support of another professional. I chose to see another EFT Practitioner because I had been working with EFT for many years with my clients and I felt comfortable with it but there are various other therapists, counselors, and modalities out there to choose from.

My grief journey is still ongoing and probably will be until the day I die but I am learning to put the broken bits of my life back together in a different way.

Part of my healing journey is to help others walking a similar path.

I must reiterate that grief cannot be healed; it can only be acknowledged, absorbed, carried, experienced, loved and cared for.

Always remember you are never on your own.

Some days I feel like I am making you proud and honouring your memory. Some days I feel heavy with heartache and lost in this world without you.

FORMS OF THERAPY

- Adlerian therapy
- Art therapy
- Behavioural therapy
- Cognitive analytic therapy (CAT)
- Cognitive behavioural therapy (CBT)
- Cognitive therapy
- Creative therapy
- Eclectic counselling
- Existential therapy
- Eye movement desensitisation and reprocessing (EMDR)
- Emotional Freedom Techniques (EFT) Tapping Therapy
- Family therapy
- Gestalt therapy
- Humanistic therapy
- Hypnotherapy
- Integrative counselling
- Interpersonal therapy
- Jungian therapy
- Matrix-Reimprinting
- Neuro-linguistic programming (NLP)

- Person-centred therapy
- Phenomenological therapy
- Play therapy
- Primal therapy
- Psychoanalysis
- Psychosynthesis
- Relationship therapy
- Solution-focused brief therapy
- Transactional analysis

It is important that you connect with your therapist or practitioner and that you feel safe and comfortable with them. You do not need to understand the particular process they use but you do need to trust them.

HUMAN BEING VERSUS HUMAN DOING

In a fast-paced world that has a twenty-four hour news and connection through social media at all times, most people feel like they are constantly playing catch up.

I used to spend most of my time being busy. I would feel guilty if I sat down in the middle of the day to read a book because there might be ironing to do and there was always a meal to prepare. My mind was constantly thinking about what needed to be done, whether it was the housework, or another blog to write, or a new project, I had this need to keep busy. The only time I allowed myself to relax was on holiday and only then if I was on a beach. I could still be busy on holiday as there were places to visit and experiences to have. I was always on the go.

Losing Matthew forced me to stop. I could not do anything else. The wind had been well and truly knocked out of me and I was on my knees. The world I knew had crashed down around me, and I was in the vortex of deep, deep grief. It did not matter if there was a pile of ironing, and we didn't feel like eating so there were no meals to prepare. My creative juices had stopped flowing and I lost interest in any projects.

Life after loss looks very different. The world you once knew has been turned upside down, cracked open, broken into tiny pieces, and shaken up. Where do you start?

I often look to nature for the answers. A walk in nature is an opportunity to breathe in deeply and notice the stillness. I turn off my phone and allow myself to be present in the fresh air. There is no twenty-four-hour news or connection to social media in nature. Nature continues to be nature as it weathers all storms teaching us to weather ours too.

We don't need to be busy. Being busy speeds up time and then we wonder why there are not enough hours in a day. We don't need to defend our life in terms of productivity.

Rest is an essential part of living.

Time slows down the more you rest, and adequate rest activates the parasympathetic nervous system. This helps your body to activate its inner healing and return to a state of homeostasis. This is when your body can repair and recover.

When the battery runs low on your phone and tablet, you recharge them but sadly, many of us don't realise we can do the same for ourselves with a little rest.

Allow rest to be part of your grief.

Take out 15-20 mins every day to just sit and rest. recharge your battery,

notice the tick of the clock,
the soft humming of the fridge,
or the birds singing,
the sound of traffic,
your heartbeat,
your breath as it enters and leaves your body,
or just the silence.

It took the loss of my son for me to learn the importance of resting.

Resting is being.

Resting is doing.

"Shhhhh, silence is the language of the angels!"

HAVING A CRY FEST

For some, crying can be incredibly hard and there may be various reasons why it is difficult. Maybe you were bought up in a family or a culture that didn't encourage you to express your feelings and emotions. Maybe you were told, big boys don't cry.

Many well-meaning parents discouraged displays of emotion especially from their sons, but boys and men feel the same range of emotions as their female counterparts. The notion that women are more emotional is a myth. For decades it has simply been more socially acceptable for women to show emotions, while the men were conditioned not to. This is helpful to no one. We need to teach our sons to express their emotions so we can raise a generation of men who are more self-aware and emotionally connected.

Maybe you do not give yourself permission to cry because you feel you will lose control. Tears wash away our pain but if you find it difficult to allow the tears to flow, it's okay, just consider the following:

You will be able to stop once you start.
It will not make you feel worse.
It is a self-healing act.

It is healthy to cry.
It is a release.
Feeling is healing.
You will not lose control.

If you find it hard to cry, maybe you could try listening to a song that makes you feel sad. While listening to that song really connect to the lyrics and allow yourself to feel moved by the music. Music can be very healing. Whether you choose a song that makes you feel uplifted or whether you want a cry fest, either way is healing. You may feel washed out after a good cry, but this will pass. Give yourself permission to feel it and let it out. It is part of the healing process.

"There is a voice that doesn't use words. Listen." Rumi

MESSAGE FROM A LOVED ONE

I hear you. I feel you. I see you.
When you smile and laugh, it sends me peace.
No, you couldn't have saved me.
No, you couldn't have done more.
Yes, you made the right decision.
Promise me that you will love with all your heart,
forgive in ways you thought impossible, release anger that
no longer serves you, let go of guilt as it was never
required, and only be sad for a while.
The bond we share cannot be broken because love is
infinite.
Until we meet again, honour my death by finding
peace.
Thank you.
I love you.

TYPES OF GRIEF

I am including the following information in this book because I found it extremely helpful to understand the various types of grief. When you appreciate that there are different types of grief, this can help you to process and understand your experience. Learning about the various types of grief certainly helped me. I hope it helps you too. I could probably write a chapter on each one but for the purpose of this book I have just clarified a brief overview.

Normal Grief

What a stupid name for this grief! I prefer to call it regular grief. Regular grief is a normal part of human suffering. If someone goes through life without experiencing regular grief, they are very lucky. With regular grief people will experience the waves of emotion as they process their grief and over time, it will diminish. They will still feel sad when they think about their loss and they will always miss their loved ones, but they will be able to move forward in a meaningful way without becoming stuck in the grieving process.

When my elderly mother passed away aged ninety it felt so incredibly sad. Dementia had stolen mum over the years, but she was still my mum. I became her main carer, and I loved my role. During this time, we had some very special moments which I will be eternally grateful for but when she passed away peacefully it felt like a happy release. It was still emotional and still a shock, even though I knew it was coming. Our parents are supposed to die before us, it is the natural order of life and death, but it still hurts. It doesn't matter how old our loved ones are when they die, we are never ready to lose them, and nothing can prepare us for that moment. When I think about mum now, I still feel sad and I miss her, but I feel that I am experiencing normal / regular grief over her passing. My father died back in 2008 and looking back now I realise that I experienced regular grief over him too. He was in his early eighties, but he had been ill for many years. Losing both my parents left a big hole but I am able to function and live my life in a full and meaningful way without them. This is regular grief.

Anticipatory Grief

You may experience anticipatory grief when a loved one or close friend has been diagnosed with a terminal illness or has been put on end-of-life / palliative care. Watching a loved one deteriorate in front of your eyes is torture and it is normal to feel hopeless and helpless. I experienced anticipatory grief watching my son Matthew fade away due to his illness. It was out of my control and there was nothing I could do to stop him from dying (although my God I tried everything). You want to reassure your loved one that everything will be okay but when you cannot do this, it is your worst nightmare. I remember how my crazy thoughts used to take me into dark places and I used to think about the future. A future without him - without all the medical interventions, endless hospital appointments, ambulances, scans, blood tests, the constant anxiety of not knowing what the next day would bring. I felt guilty when I thought about his death. I am his mum and I am supposed to save him and keep him safe. Yes, I was an expert in anticipatory grief!

Thoughts race through your mind.

Will their death be peaceful?
Will it happen in hospital or at home?
How am I going to cope?
Will they suffer?

This is your minds way of coming to terms and preparing yourself for the inevitable. This scenario can bring a type of relief when death does steal your loved one. This can then be followed by guilt and other types of grief.

Delayed Grief
Delayed grief can be caused by growing up in a culture or environment that discourages grieving. It can also be due to feeling like you should not grieve for the person, and you suppress the emotions even from yourself. You put up a mental wall around your feelings so they cannot overwhelm you. Also, this delayed reaction could happen because you are not able to cope with the emotional weight of your grief or the reality of your loss right away. Maybe you were incredibly young, or your loss may have happened in a traumatic or sudden way.

My big brother Stephen died suddenly when I was eleven years old, and I can relate to delayed grief. I had never experienced grief before and it was years later that I really experienced the sadness of losing my brother. I remember being more upset for my parents at the time as they were constantly sad. As a child to see your parents grieving can be quite traumatic. They did try to hide their emotions to protect us, but I remember their muffled conversations and stifled sobs to shield me and my siblings from their sadness. I probably grew up suppressing my emotions because of this. A lot of people do not know how to deal with grief, and they stumble through in the best way they can, but remember, everyone is just doing their best.

Complicated Grief

Complicated grief is also known as prolonged grief disorder. About 10 - 20% of people grieving experience this. This type of grief does not wane over time. Grief can be complicated, for example when the deceased is an estranged parent. Also complicated grief can be worsened by the inability to accept the death of a loved one and it is easy to get stuck in grief. There are many types of therapies available to help people move through the process, but it is important to recognise when you feel stuck. Grief cannot be rushed, and everyone moves through at different times but if you feel stuck then it is important to reach out and ask for help. I work as a therapist and at first, I didn't ask for help. I knew all the techniques and various ways to move through grief and I thought as a therapist, I can do this on my own. I was being stubborn but also part of me felt uncomfortable about seeing another therapist. A therapist seeing a therapist! If I was any good as a therapist, then why couldn't I sort myself out? Sometimes we just have to admit that we need help. It was only when I reached out for help that I managed to move forward, one tiny step at a time.

Disenfranchised Grief

Disenfranchised grief occurs when you lack social recognition or societal support for your loss. It is also known as hidden grief or sorrow. Perinatal losses and elective abortions are not talked about or acknowledged but these experiences bring their own grief.

You may experience disenfranchised grief after the loss of a personality from dementia, or the loss of a loved one who is not a blood relative for example, a boyfriend/girlfriend, extramarital lover, or in-law.

Many pet owners often feel disenfranchised grief at the loss of their pet, as they grieve deeply but also feel they cannot take time off work, or do not know who to talk to about the way they feel. Our pets are part of our family but not everyone understands particularly people who do not own pets.

Disenfranchised grief occurs anytime someone feels that society has denied their need to grieve.

Those experiencing disenfranchised grief may feel isolated, stigmatized, and ashamed. It is important to find someone that understands your loss and how you feel.

Chronic Grief

When grief becomes prolonged it is called chronic grief and very much like complicated grief it does not reduce in severity over time. Chronic grief is experienced when acceptance of the loss does not occur. This type of grief is experienced by up to 20% of the bereaved and may cause long-term effects on both physical and mental health.

Distorted Grief

Distorted grief is characterised by extreme reactions and behavioural changes. With this type of grief, you may become angry with the world, at others, or yourself. You are more likely to become hostile, confrontational, or maybe self-harm.

Cumulative Grief

Cumulative grief builds up over time due to several deaths and losses. This is also referred to as bereavement overload or grief overload.

Exaggerated Grief

Exaggerated grief is the exaggeration of the normal /regular grieving process. The intensity of exaggerated grief can get worse over time. Hyper-grieving is another phrase to describe this type of grief. This grief is the amplification of the regular grieving process, either through negative behaviours, or poor mental health. Exaggerated grief could potentially develop into a major psychiatric disorder.

Masked Grief

Masked grief is most common among men, or in societies and cultures where the rules dictate how you must act or appear following the loss of someone close to you. Suppression of any grief is not healthy. It can cause mental illnesses and disorders as the person who is grieving does not give themselves the time or space to process their loss.

Traumatic Grief

If your loved one was murdered or killed in a terrorist attack, car crash, drowning, fire etc. you may experience traumatic grief. You will not just mourn the loss of your loved one, you may also be traumatised by it.

Collective Grief

Collective grief is a type of grieving experienced by communities or societies, for example, when Princess Diana died, a wave of collective grief swept across the planet. We also feel collective grief when we attend funerals. The communal energy of sadness is palpable.

Collective grief should also be healed collectively. Coming together to mourn and grieve publicly helps to reaffirm those ties to one another. There is a healing power in togetherness.

Inhibited Grief

Inhibited grief is when someone shows some signs of grieving, but not to the level or intensity expected based on the relationship that has been lost. There may also be versions of masked grief or delayed grief in this scenario. It may be that they are trying to be strong for everyone else, so they constrain their emotions to protect others. I certainly displayed inhibited grief. I never used to be a public crier, but I also felt I needed to be strong for my family particularly my elderly mum. Grief has changed me and I cry at anything now. I even cry at adverts on the television these days! I've realised that tears are a release and I allow them to fall whenever they need to. For some, inhibiting grief is a conscious decision as they choose to keep their grief private and this must be respected; although it is important that they allow themselves to grieve in private.

Abbreviated Grief

Abbreviated grief is a short-lived grief in which the person who is grieving feels like they should, or they move on quickly. It could be due to insufficient attachment (not enough affection, connection) to the deceased person. This could be true of children who barely knew a distant relative, or estranged parent. Perhaps a widow or widower has remarried rather quickly, immediately replacing their partner. It is important to remember there are no rules to grief and everyone does it differently.

Absent Grief

Absent grief is defined as there being no grief after the death of a loved one. Many people who have been the main caregivers for their loved ones may experience this type of grief. This can happen when a person has grieved so much already (anticipatory grief) that they may experience a sense of relief when their loved one dies. It may be days, weeks, months, or even years before they start to fully experience their loss.

Ambiguous Grief

Examples of ambiguous loss include kidnapping and missing bodies due to war, terrorism, ethnic cleansing, genocide, and natural disasters such as earthquake, flood, and tsunami. Experiencing an ambiguous loss can lead to personal questions, such as, "Am I still married to my missing spouse?" Ambiguous loss can be the loss of psychological mind. "Am I still a child to a parent who no longer remembers me?"

Happy Guilt!

Accept that good days come with guilt.

After a while and it's different for everyone, you will have moments of happiness such as:

- Daydreaming or reminiscing about something that makes you feel good.
- Laughing out loud at something funny.
- Enjoying time with family or friends.

Happy guilt happens when something takes you out of the grief vortex for a short period of time and then you realise you didn't feel grief stricken for a moment or maybe even a few minutes. Then it hits you, the happy guilt, like a tsunami of, "Crap! How could I forget my grief"?

Once the initial rawness of grief becomes dulled, we find ourselves moving into guilt. Grief and guilt often walk hand in hand. One day we realise we are smiling and then laughing at something. For a moment, our minds move to something other than our grief. Then the guilt of feeling happy for a fleeting moment overwhelms us. You ask yourself:

"How can I be happy?"
"How can I enjoy life?"
"Does this mean I'm forgetting?"
"How can I laugh again?"

After they die, it feels wrong to breathe, to dream, to laugh, to smile, to hope, to wish - but it would feel more wrong to spend eternity explaining to them why you stopped living.

You have the right to feel happy. Happiness is not limited to people who are not grieving. Joy can be found even in the saddest of times. Let me repeat that. There is joy even in the saddest of times.

I can be both happy and sad at the same time. It's a new skill!

Both joy and sadness can dwell within us and if we allow them both the space they deserve, we can live well within that balance. Give yourself the space and permission to grieve deeply and be sad but to also enjoy moments of happiness, joy, and laughter too. Accept that guilt needs to be loved and cared for. It is part of you and it needs to be processed.

You did enough!

You couldn't save them!

Appreciate that your nervous system needs a break. When you are grieving, a flood of neurochemicals and hormones can potentially disrupt delicate balances within the body leading to specific symptoms, such as disturbed sleep, loss of appetite, fatigue and anxiety. Having moments of joy and happiness amidst your grief is allowed and actually very good for you. Give yourself permission to enjoy them.

Happy guilt has a sneaky way of catching you out. Even years later, happy guilt can pull at your heart strings. This is a normal part of grief, and it cannot be avoided. You can breathe deeply through these moments and remind yourself that it is because you loved and lost a special person. Would this person want you to feel this way? You can acknowledge the happy guilt, thank it, then give yourself permission to let it go.

Each grief wave or tsunami which washes over you is another reminder of your loss, but I repeat, you did enough. You couldn't save them.

Psychologists and psychotherapists are classifying more and more different types of grief as time goes by. They like labels and there is an idea that naming is taming. It is helpful to appreciate and acknowledge the various types of grief and maybe some of the descriptions above resonate with you but remember that whatever you are feeling is not wrong and it doesn't need a label. Also, be mindful that it is possible to experience a few different types of grief over the same loss.

Grief in any form can potentially lead on to depression and other mental health issues, including PTSD (post-traumatic stress disorder).

Although it is useful to be aware of the various types of grief, I personally prefer to not put myself in a box. For me it is important to just notice how I feel from one moment to the next without putting any logic or labels on it. I do feel that labels in any form can give grief more power.

Everyone is different so it is important to experience grief your way. Your way is right for you. If you feel you are not coping well, you can enlist the support of a grief specialist. You do not need to cope on your own. Please speak to your doctor, therapist, or counsellor for guidance. It is important to acknowledge your feelings and not rush through the early stages of grief. Please allow yourself to feel what you feel and be gentle with yourself and know that it will change. If you feel stuck, reach out and seek help. You may just need a gentle nudge, or empathetic ear, or a compassionate friend to loosen your grief.

Early grief may make you feel like a massive hole has opened in your body and / or that part of you is missing. The pain can feel unbearable and nothing you do can take it away.

As you navigate your way through the grief journey you will find it comes in waves. When you feel overwhelmed by an emotional wave, notice how it makes you feel and observe the sensations inside. Sit with it. Allow yourself to feel it. Do not push it away or suppress it. It is important to acknowledge your grief in order for you to process it. Feeling is healing!

Grief can be triggered even decades later. You can be okay one minute and in bits the next, but this is how grief works.

Grief is proof you loved a special person.

Tears are love in liquid form and they help to wash away the pain.

Maybe you are reading this and feeling guilty because you actually feel okay. Grief doesn't always have to be breaking down, constantly crying, feeling lost and empty. It is okay to feel okay too.

It is okay to not be okay and it is okay to be okay! There are no rules!

Mourning

Mourning is the outward expression of grief. It is the external symbol of rituals and customs to show respect to the person or people who have died. Some cultures expect a dignified and quiet response to the loss while in other societies mourners are expected to openly display their raw emotions. In some cultures, those in mourning tend to wear white to represent the passing of an individual, while in other cultures black or dark-coloured clothes are worn. The wearing of a black armband and the hanging of flags at half-mast are other ways for the community to support the bereaved. Mourning is a sign of collective respect which can bring comfort to those closest to the deceased.

You have survived this far - hold on.
It can't get any worse - this is as bad as it gets.
Stop beating yourself up - you are a work in progress.
You are transforming – stay!

TYPES OF LOSS

"Love knows not its own depth until the hour of separation"
Khahil Gibran

All deaths are sudden no matter how gradual the dying process may be.

The most painful losses are those we loved deeply. The more intense the relationship we had with our loved one, the more intense we feel the loss. Grief will be proportionate to how much space we held in our hearts for our loved ones. It can be described as losing a limb but as you process your grief you learn to move forward without this part of you and you grow around your grief.

I could write a whole chapter on each type of loss but for the purpose of this book, I have written a summary of each one.

Types of loss include:

Spouse/partner - A common theme among people who have experienced this type of loss is a feeling like you have lost an essential part of yourself.

Child - No parent expects to face the death of a child and no grandparent expects to lose a grandchild. The death of a child goes against the natural order we expect life to follow. The agony of losing a child of any age is unbearable.

Sibling – Brothers and sisters interact whether they are connecting, conspiring, or bickering and no -one else understands the family dynamics as much as another sibling. The death of a sibling not only changes the family forever, but it changes the relationship with the parents and the other siblings.

Parent - Losing a parent can be a terrible thing to go through at any age. Ideally our parents should pass peacefully in their old age but even this way does not protect people from experiencing the pain of loss.

Grandparent – The death of a grandparent is felt by the many generations within the family unit and this loss can feel huge. Even though it is natural to die in old age, it may not make the process of grief any easier.

Other family members – The loss of any family member is incredibly sad but depending on how close you were to the person determines how you will experience your loss.

Miscarriage - most women agree that the emotional trauma of shock and grief are far worse than the physical effects of miscarriage. People talk less about miscarriage than any other loss.

Stillborn - Stillbirth is when a baby dies before she or he is born, at more than 24 weeks of pregnancy. Some people like to describe this experience as - the baby is born sleeping. There are some wonderful charities thankfully that can support people who have experienced a miscarriage or stillborn.

Close friend –The death of a close friend can seem worse than the death of a family member. A lot depends on the type of relationship you had with the deceased. The same can be said for a classmate or colleague.

Pet –Society tends to treat pet loss as trivial and it lacks social recognition or societal support. Our pets are part of the family and when they die it leaves a massive hole. The family may grieve very deeply but feel they cannot take time off work. They may feel they cannot talk about it in the same way as other losses.

Lots of people describe how the Covid situation created feelings of loss because their lives changed so much. People experienced a type of bereavement as they longed for their pre-Covid lifestyles. The Covid deaths, the jobs that people lost, the businesses that went under, the homes that were lost, the celebrations that were postponed, the ordinary lives that we were used to, gone. All those things and more are affecting us at some level. During this time, we were not allowed to visit relatives in care homes. We were not always allowed to spend time with a dying loved one in hospital. We lost our freedoms. We were limited to how many people could attend funerals. These experiences can further complicate any type of grief and loss.

The breakdown of a relationship is a type of bereavement and this needs processing in the same way.

You can also grieve the loss of your health; you miss the person you were before the illness or diagnosis.

There are so many reasons why people experience grief and loss, but it is important to acknowledge and respect each individual case.

Some people have no idea what to say and may say the clumsiest words but be kind, they are probably doing their best to support you. When Matthew died, it annoyed me that others compared my loss to them losing their grandparents or their pet dog or cat. How dare they compare my son to their pet or 95-year-old grandparent, but they had no idea what it felt like to lose a child. I appreciate now that their intentions were good. I understand that they just wanted to try and connect with me in some way. They were reaching out to me in the best way they knew, explaining to me that they had also experienced a loss. It is true that shared experiences can bring a type of fellowship and compassion.

Grief wars.
I know the loss of a pet hamster is sad, but maybe not as sad as losing a dog, or cat, but not as sad as losing an elderly parent. Each loss is unique and so is the griever. It is important we respect and appreciate that we do not know how others experience their loss, just as we cannot expect people to understand how we experience ours. No-one else can possibly know or understand what you are going through. Understand and accept that. Loss is loss – try not to compare.

"Don't run away from grief, o' soul - Look for the remedy inside the pain, because the rose came from the thorn and the ruby came from a stone". Rumi

DO NOT STAND AT MY GRAVE AND WEEP

Do not stand at my grave and weep
I am not there. I do not sleep.
I am a thousand winds that blow.
I am the diamond glints on snow.
I am the sunlight on ripened grain.
I am the gentle autumn rain.
When you awaken in the morning's hush
I am the swift uplifting rush
Of quiet birds in circled flight.
I am the soft stars that shine at night.
Do not stand at my grave and cry.
I am not there.
I did not die.

Mary Elizabeth Frye

MOVING FORWARD

Moving forward is about carrying the grief and learning to coexist with it. It takes time to accept that life is different now but different can be okay. Give yourself permission to grow and transform and accept that this is a different version of you.

I am still growing around my grief. I feel like I am an updated version of computer software, but as with any new system, I come with gremlins. Perhaps I am still not even sure who this new person is yet. I have new insecurities with this update, and it may take time to feel totally comfortable with who I am. I have an inner knowing that I am going in the right direction and that life is now unfolding in a different way for me. It is my new reality. Do I like it? If I say "yes", then it sounds like life is better now without my son Matthew and if I say "no" it sounds like I am resisting it, and what we resist persists, so I am learning to accept it.

As I bring this book to a close, I reflect on how far I have come. I am still a work in progress, but I will continue to share my love and light with anyone who needs support. It is my life purpose and retirement is not on the cards.

I do not know who I would be without my experiences, good and bad, and I am learning to be grateful for them all. *"How can you be grateful for losing your son I hear you scream?"* (Big sigh!) I look for the positives in everything and maybe, just maybe, Matthew and I created a soul plan before we incarnated into our physical bodies. Maybe we communicated about our human journeys on how best we could be a light in the darkness for others. Was his illness and death at the age of twenty-seven part of that plan? He touched many people through his inspiring, brave blog (www.matt-bates.co.uk) and our family is so very proud of him. Sharing my grief with the world through my work and my books has helped thousands of people and maybe that was part of my purpose. Maybe, just maybe, Matthew chose to be the catalyst for that. That is what I feel is true in my heart and we continue to make a great partnership.

My daughter is my biggest guru, and she continues to teach me earthly stuff while Matthew teaches me about life after loss and soul level stuff. I am a mum to two incredible souls one thankfully still on this earth plane and one on the other side. How lucky am I? Can you see where my gratitude comes from now? This was not what I had planned, but I have accepted, this is my life.

I am learning to live my life in a more contented, peaceful, spiritual way. Feeling appreciation for everything that comes my way, good or bad. Seeing difficulties as opportunities to learn and grow. Making my family proud. Making Matthew proud. I still miss him dreadfully every day, and that is okay, but I am able to move forward carrying my grief, accepting my grief, caring for my grief, and making peace with my grief and most importantly, loving my grief!

When we make peace with our grief, I believe this sends our loved ones peace too.

This is how I do grief. This is the right way for me and how you do yours is the right way for you. We are all just doing our best to survive and thrive.

You do not have to be religious or spiritual to make peace with your grief. You can be an atheist, agnostic or anything you want to be. Whatever belief system you choose, you can put in the work but no one else can do it for you.

When I am having a sad moment or tough day, I accept that it's okay to not be okay! I know it will pass. I like to remind myself that my track record for getting through the bad days is 100%.

Sometimes I remind myself of how I would like my loved ones to feel when I'm gone. I appreciate there will be a time for being sad, to grieve, etc. I have to admit I am pretty amazing, and I will be missed; but after a while and it is different for everyone, I want my loved ones to honour my life by living their best life. There will be sad moments and that is okay, but I want my loved ones to remember me wild swimming and paddle boarding (I do love water). Remember the laughs (I do like a laugh) and I have actually pee'd myself laughing many times. Remember my piano or accordion playing (or maybe not as it was never that great). Remember me as the mad hedgehog lady, (I do love hedgehogs). Remember the good times. The good memories will be the gifts I leave behind. If my loved ones do not remember this stuff I will come back and haunt them!

Grieving can make you feel isolated but remember you are not on your own. If you feel you are, please reach out and contact me.

I am sending you so much love and support as you navigate yourself through your bereavement. Whether you choose to be dragged through kicking and screaming, or whether you do it privately, normally, abnormally, whichever way, that is the right way for you.

Please do feel free to get in touch and share your experience.
Let me know if this book has helped you in anyway.
I would love to hear from you.
I wish you well on your journey.
Lots of love and hugs.
Louise Xx

"Go back and take care of yourself.
Your body needs you, your feelings need you, your perceptions need you.
Your suffering needs you to acknowledge it.
Go home and be there for all these things."
Thich Nhat Hanh

Table Of Contents

Printed in Great Britain
by Amazon

29264234R00126